Landlord Away Your Student Loan Debt

Michael O'Dell

Printed by CreateSpace.

Available from Amazon.com and other book stores.

EBook available on Kindle.

Audio version available from Audible.

This book is dedicated to my wife, Lela and our children, Daniel, Niles and Rose.

Table of Contents:

Chapter 1: WTF?   1

Chapter 2: Student Loan Strategies   3

Chapter 3: An Opportunity   13

Chapter 4: My First Mistake   17

Chapter 5: Stumbling Across Experience   21

Chapter 6: It Was a Dark and Stormy Night   27

Chapter 7: These Real Estate Books Work!   37

Chapter 8: Caveat Emptor   41

Chapter 9: You're Gonna Get Shot!   45

Chapter 10: This House Needs a Priest, Not a
Contractor   49

Chapter 12: The Banks These Days   63

Chapter 13: No Pay, No Stay   69

Chapter 14: Shake and Bake   75

Chapter 15: A Copy of a Copy   79

Chapter 16: Section 8 is Great!*   **83**

Chapter 17: Narrowing it All Down   **93**

Chapter 18: Getting Money   **105**

Chapter 19: Tips to Keep You Sane   **109**

Chapter 20: The End?   **125**

Bibliography   **131**

iv

Preface

This book is about getting out of debt by using more debt. Yes, I said it. You can borrow your way out of debt. Not by taking one loan and paying off another, but by borrowing money to buy houses that generate enough income to cover multiple debts. The rental income from a strategically purchased home will pay for itself and still have money left over to cover other expenses.

My strategy can be utilized to eliminate any debt you may have, or to simply make you rich. I focus on student loans in this book because they were the primary reason I began this endeavor. Anyone can get into real estate, and becoming a landlord is quite easy. The devil is in the details. That's why I wrote a book, not a pamphlet.

If you aren't in student loan debt, then good for you! Just skip Chapter Two and read on. This book will give you lots of insight into the world of land-lording and how to enter it with nothing out of your own pocket.

If you are in student loan debt, then you are the kind of risk taker who should be reading this book! You made a calculated risk to go into debt to improve your financial situation. After analyzing the numbers, you decided to further yourself sooner rather than saving money for decades to pay for college. You thought it out, right? It would be easier to pay off student loan debt with a higher income than it would be to save for college with a lower paycheck. The decision to borrow became simple. You didn't hesitate to sign those loan forms, did you? The math made sense, and you pulled the trigger. You gambler.

I would like to present you with a new calculated risk. Becoming a landlord is certainly a gamble. If you jump into real estate uneducated and unprepared, you can lose everything. But if you educate and prepare yourself before you start out, the odds change direction and go in your favor. When I tell people what I do, many folks stop me and say, "Whoa now, that's a lot of risk you take! I can't do that." If you are thinking along those lines, then answer me this: You weren't guaranteed to graduate college were you? Surely you thought about that scenario more than once while you were still in school. You probably thought something like, "If I quit or flunk, I'll be worse off than ever!" Oh the dread to be back at square one but now in horrible debt! That thought helped push me through while I was in school, in too deep to turn back. I bet you felt the same way from time to time. Those student loans you took on weren't a sure thing. Nothing is. So get over it, open your mind, and hear me out.

I wish this book would have existed when I started landlording. That's why I created this work. I want to help you do the same thing I did. Furthermore, I'm going to walk you down the path I took and give you the wisdom of my hindsight so you don't make the same mistakes I did.

This book was originally written as an eBook with active hyperlinks. Instead of listing hyperlinks, I will indicate some keywords to search for in your web browser of choice. I have no intention of steering you toward any websites that charge a fee for their services. If you run across a predatory site that wants your credit card information, keep searching down the list.

A lot of effort has gone into making this book an "easy read." I purposefully left out as much business, landlording, and real estate jargon as possible. The approach taken assumes the reader is not a seasoned landlord, nor an expert regarding student loans.

Far from a compendium of knowledge, this book is meant to be a firm starting off point. If you decide to enter the world of landlording, you will benefit from a library of information written by people from a variety of backgrounds.

It should go without saying, but I'm going to say it anyway: This book does not provide legal advice or financial advice. If you become a landlord, you face the risk of losing money, getting sued, or, at very least, getting mad at people. You also face the risk of making a bunch of money. So let's get started.

Introduction

This book chronicles the path I took, which made every student loan payment for me, and put a few bucks in my pocket to boot. I didn't win the lottery or cheat the system. Everything I did was legal and ethical. My strategy was simple: Pay off student loan debt with real estate.

I have never made a student loan payment with my own money. I'm sorry to say I don't have any gimmicky system to sell you. If you read this book, then start your journey and stick to it, you will easily be able to own more houses than me. You will get renters to help you pay off your debt and buy you houses - all while saying, "Thank you!"

My wife and I managed to turn an idea into five houses that will pay for themselves in a relatively short period of time. The rental income derived from these houses is not only rapidly buying them, it is also covering our monthly student loan bills. We accomplished this without using any of our own money! We turned paying our student loans into a game, and I smile every month when the money is drafted out of an account that I didn't fund. Yes, we're in more debt than ever, but *we don't feel it*, because one large debt (real estate) is paying itself off while simultaneously paying off another large debt (student loans). And when that game is played out, we have a perpetual, substantial income that will scale up with inflation as long as we care to be landlords. Rent never goes down, now does it?

Some things to keep in mind:

- You can do it!

- The main quality that successful real estate investors possess is *determination*.

- Real estate investing does not require any skills that are hard to learn, nor any innate abilities you don't already have.

- Don't listen to naysayers! They have talked themselves out of buying houses for one reason or another and have convinced themselves that their uninformed opinion is right. The majority of people fall into this category. That's fine. If everyone were a landlord, the market would be saturated, and you wouldn't be able to make any money.

- The market is not, and never will be, saturated with landlords. You are not going up against hundreds of bloodthirsty, amoral scam artists clamoring over a deal. You are buying a cheap house. Our used minivan cost more than any rental I've ever bought.

- Most people don't want to see you succeed. They have decided that what you are about to do is impossible, a fool's errand. You can't change their mind any more than they can change yours.

- Surround yourself with those who have done it and want you to get there. These people exist, are nearby, easy to find, and want to meet you.

- Things will come out differently than you originally thought. If this is your first landlording book, congratulations! Keep an open mind. You are entering an amazing world.

- It took you years to get your college degree, it won't take you that long to get started in real estate. Of course it will take you years to become an expert, but you don't need expert level knowledge to become a landlord.

- The "work" of getting a real estate education will be almost effortless. You will become driven to learn this stuff. This is an endeavor that you are undertaking for yourself. Unlike studying for some of those lame college classes, you will become obsessed with learning about real estate.

Also, unlike the "work" you do at work, becoming a landlord is a long term moneymaker for you alone. You decide when to work, what you do, and how you do it. You will be your own boss and will find yourself thinking like a boss.

- Keep your long term goals in mind, they will get you through any short term difficulties. It's going to take a long time to pay those loans back, but who cares? As long as you aren't making the payments with your own money, it's all good!

I went to grad school to advance my career and raise my income. I thought tripling my Registered Nurse salary would make me rich and I'd have it made. But come to find out, the higher pay comes with considerably more expenses. I'm in a brave new income tax bracket, and all those write offs you get when you make $50K are GONE after you break $100K. Sure I'm making good money, but the student loan debt required to get us to this point is crippling. Between my wife and me, we graduated with over $250,000.00 in debt to the federal government. We had a kid and another one on the way. We simply wanted to live in a decent neighborhood and, six months out of school, the first payment on that staggering debt came due. I had a very expensive college education, but it didn't prepare me for the freight train heading our way.

I use "we" and "I" interchangeably throughout this book. The idea to do this was expressly mine, and I was the one who implemented the majority of actions. But there was no way I could have pulled this off without the consent and support of my wife. She has been by my side throughout this process which, at times, has been very stressful. She's been there to tell me things were going to be alright when I was doubting myself, and as time goes on, (and our kids get bigger) she has been more and more involved with the process. She helped me write this book, too!

Chapter 1: WTF?

When our first student loan bills hit, we were shocked. My minimum payment was scheduled to be $2,500.00 per month for 10 YEARS! My wife's payments were going to be $900.00 for the same amount of time! Although the federal government sets their own interest rate to borrow money at 0%, they picked ours to be 7.8%. Of the $3,400.00 payments, $1,800.00 per month was going to **INTEREST** alone. If you took my income after tax and subtracted our student loan bill, it busted me back down to what I was bringing home as a Registered Nurse. I am now doing anesthesia for a living, and being broke for the next ten years was certainly not part of the plan. We had babies, and my wife was planning on being home with them while they were little, so my income was all we had to work with. I get pretty cranky after I exceed 40 work hours a week, and I wanted to be at home as much as possible so I could be part of my kids' childhood. The last thing either of us wanted was me working all the time, only home on the occasional weekend like a long haul trucker.

I called the number on my student loan bill, and I told the person on the other end of the line that I couldn't afford to make payments that high. I asked if there were some kind of payment plan I could get on. "No." said the hostile voice on the other end of the line. "If you couldn't afford to make these payments, you shouldn't have borrowed the money in the first place!" I felt like I had just been sold into slavery. He told me my only option was to pay the full amount or go into forbearance. He explained that forbearance was a grace period wherein you can skip payments, but interest continues to accrue. There is a lifetime maximum of 12 monthly payments you may skip on your student loans. I told him to sign me up. There was no way I could make the payments and I would think of something in the coming year. The federal loan representative then said, "Do you realize that the interest on your account will continue to accrue, and after a year you will owe us an additional $18,000.00+?" I told him he might as well make it $20,000.00. What was the difference? The debt was so huge it didn't matter how much I really owed. It wasn't until much later that I learned he was wrong, and that my ignorance was working against me.

For an additional $18,000.00 of debt, I bought us a year. But I could have been in a much better position if I knew the system.

If you haven't already, you need to consolidate your federal loans and explore your repayment options. Minimizing your monthly payments makes it a lot easier for your tenants to cover your bills! In the next chapter I'll go over some options worth considering.

Chapter 2: Student Loan Strategies

If you just graduated, you will notice that you have an array of "smaller" loans. Most student loans are individually issued each semester and start accruing interest as soon as they are issued to you. While in school, you are not expected to make payments and are therefore on academic forbearance. Forbearance simply means you are not required to make payments. Interest accrues whether you pay or not, so you get a notice every quarter regarding the additional debt that is piling on against you, and they ask if you want to pay that down. I never paid while still in school, I had to live off my loans, and making interest payments with borrowed money seemed like a waste of time.

After graduation, the first order of business is to consolidate your student loans into one impressively large debt. Consolidation is a simple, one time only process. You apply for consolidation online and your federal loans all become "paid in full" and combined into one large loan with one interest rate.   You can find this link online by searching for "Federal Consolidation Loan." Now, there are several predatory websites that want to charge you money for this free service. If you run across a website that wants your credit card number you are in the wrong place. Don't expect a good deal on the new interest rate, the government will combine all your balances and average the interest rates for your various loans to arrive at the new figures. For some reason, the consolidation process takes a month or more to be finalized. So, if you are really wanting to drag out your repayment, you can get an extra month of administrative forbearance if you time things right. I'll give you a theoretical example of drawing out the time to repayment later.

I didn't have to start off in forbearance! The representative I spoke to the day I called about a repayment plan really led me astray. It's incredible how uninformed I was when I started the repayment period for my student loans. There are actually a few different repayment plans to choose from. If you couldn't, or didn't work while you were in school, and you get on an income based repayment plan, you can get credit for a year's worth of payments without having to make a payment! I'm not advocating irresponsible behavior here, but it is *expensive* to start over, and many people have to move a significant distance to begin their career. Having only six months to make your first payment is very little time.

The federal government has several repayment plans to choose from depending on the types of loans you have. Search online for "Fed Loan Payment Plans," yet again heeding my advice about predatory websites. The income based repayment plans are very similar to each other. Loan payments are based on your income from the previous year. If you haven't paid your loans entirely after making 20 - 25 years of on time payments (depending on the plan), your remaining debt is forgiven. Keep this in mind: If you follow through with an income based repayment plan and have

4

a substantial balance forgiven by the government, that forgiven amount is considered *income*. You will be hit by a huge tax bill the year forgiveness is granted, however, the tax bill will be far less than what it would cost you to pay your full loan balance. Talk to a tax professional and start preparing a few years before your loan is forgiven. One sweet thing about landlording your way out of debt is you should own a bunch of houses outright by the time the tax man comes. Sell a property or two (keeping in mind you will recapture depreciation - another tax zinger) to pay the federal government back. You still didn't spend any of your own money!

The way the government calculates your payments on an income based repayment plan is simple. Your payments are based on your "disposable income." To calculate disposable income, find the federal poverty guideline (income) for your household size in your state. To find yours, search online for "Federal poverty guidelines." Multiply your poverty guideline by 150% to arrive at your minimum required income. Now take your Adjusted Gross Income from your federal tax return and subtract your minimum required income. The resulting number is your Disposable Income. The government has decided that your student loan payments (under an income driven repayment plan) should not be more than 10% of your disposable income. So, take your disposable income, knock the last whole number off and divide by 12 to figure your monthly payment.

Example:

Let's say you are a family of three from Kansas in 2015 and your adjusted gross income (AGI) is $75,000.00 per year. The federal poverty guideline for a family that size in one of the contiguous 48 states is $20,090.00 per year.

So, $20,090.00(poverty) x 1.5 = $31,350.00 (minimum required income)

Now $75,000.00(AGI) - $31,350.00 (minimum required income) =$43,650.00 (Disposable Income)

$43,650.00 (DI) x 10% = $4,365.00 (Annual Student Loan Payment)

$4,365.00 ÷ 12 months = $363.75 (Monthly Student Loan Payment)

Income based repayments are independent of the amount you owe on your loan as long as they are lower than the standard repayment set by the government. Using the above scenario and assuming a 7.75% annual percentage rate for a consolidated student loan, your breakeven point would be $31,000.00. Meaning, the payment on a federal loan for $31,000.00 at 7.75% over 10 years using the standard repayment plan would be about $372.00 per month. If you owed less than $31,000.00 and you made $75,000.00 per year, there would be no point in participating in an income based repayment plan. However, if you owed **$300,000.00** and made $75,000.00 per year, your income based payment would be the *same* as if you owed only $31,000.00.

The Public Service student Loan Forgiveness Program (PSLF) is by far the best deal when it comes to getting rid of your loans. A quick search for "PSLF" will bring you to the website. If you qualify for the PSLF plan, you are required to make the minimum income based payments for ten years. After 120 on time payments, the Federal Government will forgive the remaining balance of your student loan debt completely **tax free** as a way of thanking you for working for a public entity. A qualifying employer can be either a government agency (at the State, Federal or local level) or a non-profit organization (A non- profit organization typically has a 403b retirement plan instead of a 401k plan). PSLF is a plan put together by the Federal Government, so your employer may not even be aware that they can participate. In order to qualify, you must submit a simple two page form to your employer to verify your full time employment with them. The two page document is found on the PSLF website. Your employment needn't be to the same employer for the entire length of repayment, and broken up periods between employers still count. All time worked after January 2007 for a qualifying employer is eligible for the PSLF so, the first people to be able to take advantage of Federal forgiveness will receive this boon in 2017. I happen to work for a university hospital system, and my paychecks come from the state. I'm happily clocking in full time, racking up state benefits while on the fast track to loan forgiveness. If you are presented with a choice between employers and all other items are equal except one qualifies for this program and the other does not, it would be of great benefit for you to consider PSLF as a deciding factor.

If you want to maximize your time away from payments, and you had little or no income while going to school, then consider getting on an income based repayment plan. This style of repayment plan is based off your income tax return. If you graduated in December, then your first payment would be due in June. File your taxes by April, then submit for your repayment in May. You would want to put in for the repayment plan pretty close to your first payment due date because you must resubmit your tax data annually. If you made nothing in the year you graduated, then your student loan payments will be NOTHING for a year! The same thing would happen if you graduated in June. You would have already filed your tax return and your first payment would be the following December, so you could submit your tax information to the student loans around Thanks-giving. Your next income based calculation wouldn't be until the holidays the following year. If you are working your way to owning several houses as a landlord and need more time, you can put in for forbearance after that first year of no payments. If needed, this strategy would give you practically *two and a half years* to establish a real estate empire that can cover your loan payments. Why didn't I think of that?

Here's an outline of how to maximize your time away from payments:

Let's say you graduate in December 2019 (Your first regular payment will be due June 2020).

Watch your deadlines and submit your consolidation paperwork in May 2020 just before the cutoff date. (Administrative forbearance will kick in and give you until July or August until first payment).

Submit for Income Based Repayment once your consolidation is complete, again pushing the deadline. You can't start IBR until you have consolidated. (This will occur around August 2020, then your loan will go on Administrative Forbearance for another month. Now your first payment is due by September or October 2020).

In October 2020, your first income based repayment is due, but you submitted your tax return from April showing you made practically nothing in 2019, so your payments are close to nothing until October 2021.

Now, in October 2021 you can put in for discretionary forbearance and stretch your payments out another full year if needed. Your first significant payment on your student loan is now due in October 2022.

The preceding options only work with Federal student loans in the United States. Private loans are a different animal. With a private loan, you are dealing with the individual creditor. I have no experience with these loans and cannot speak to them. But I encourage you to negotiate the smallest monthly payment possible until you get your rental empire up and running.

If you are worrying about the tax implications of earning more money as a landlord, fret not! If you use a zero down technique to buy a house - say your parents take out a Home Equity Line Of Credit (HELOC) and give that money to you as a loan, the money you borrow from your parents is NOT taxable as income. *Borrowed money is never considered income.* If you are paying interest on the money you borrowed, the interest payments are a tax deduction. If you have to repair anything on your house, another tax deduction. If you buy office supplies, tools, materials, pay utilities, pay closing costs, pay a lawn guy, or take your banker out to lunch for a meeting - tax deductions. Then there is the magic of depreciation! The IRS treats houses as an asset that will only last a set amount of time. The tax man says a home will fully depreciate after 27.5 years, so each year they figure 1/27.5th of the purchase price of your house will be lost. If you bought your house (minus the value of your lot - dirt does not depreciate) for $27,500.00 then every year it will depreciate $1,000.00. So the first thousand dollars you get each year in rent is not counted as income. I lose a lot on paper with my rentals each year despite the fact that I make quite a bit of money on them. Everything is tax deductible to a landlord! My rentals decrease my tax bill at the end of the year. Even if you did actually "earn" money on your rentals, your proceeds would be taxed at the lowest possible level under "Passive Income*" which comes out at a far lower rate than "Earned Income". Why is this? **Because rich people own rent houses and rich people write the rules**.

*Passive income is money you earn without having to be present to receive it. Unlike earned income, which implies you go to work to earn it, passive income is a steady flow of money that comes in at regular intervals. Another difference between earned income and passive income is **earned income is limited**. You can only work so many hours in a day. **Passive income is unlimited**, if you set things in motion, you can cause money to earn more money, which earns more money, and so forth. Now, you still have to work to earn passive income. You must build a collection of money making assets, maintain them, and make sure your little money farms are running smoothly. But ideally, this doesn't take a whole lot of your time.*

I've had a couple of people accuse me of "cheating" on my loans. "If you borrowed the money, you should pay it all back." I agree. But the government still gets their money back on a repayment plan. If you make 20 years of payments, you hardly got away scot free. If I make all 240 income based payments on my loans under their current parameters, I will have paid back over $220,000.00. The government benefits from having an educated population. It's not the student's fault the cost of college has exploded. I'm not cheating anything. I play by the rules, and in a game with stakes this high, YOU BETTER KNOW THE RULES! After all, it's not cheating at Monopoly if you roll again after getting doubles, you would be a sucker not to.

Once you get your loans on track, you need to get some houses. The next few chapters cover how things unfolded for me. Along the way, I'll give you the advice I wish I'd had.

Chapter 3: An Opportunity

How the heck do normal* people end up owning 100 houses? Doesn't it take 30 years to buy a house? I can't save up enough money to buy the house I'm living in, much less five or ten more!

*Not born into wealth, people who make less than me per hour.

What's the trick?

There's no trick, just an unconventional approach. It is a very rare person that can save the kind of money it takes to buy a rent house. Blue collar tactics of scrimping money and sacrifice will never get you there. You have to find another way to get money. Do you think Donald Trump saved ten percent of his paychecks until he could buy his first skyscraper?

A friend of my Mom's was a realtor and had a lot of rent houses here in Oklahoma. Kay made a killing and had tons of free time. I started seriously talking to her when I was 18 and was really excited to get into the business of rental housing. But when you are 18, distractions are everywhere and I was going to start college, didn't have credit and…you know the rest.

I went off to college and earned my Bachelor's of Science in Nursing. Six years after initially talking to Kay about real estate, she drove me around town looking at condominiums. We found a 1000 square foot, two bedroom, and 1.5 bathroom condo for $23,500.00. The payments on the 30 year mortgage for that property were under $200.00 per month. In addition to the monthly payments, the Home Owner's Association (HOA) fees ran $100.00 per month. All together I had a nice bachelor pad for under $300.00 per month. Kay told me it would make an excellent rental property, I agreed with her and bought my first house in 1998.

In 1999 I was hired by a travel nursing company and began working for hospitals across the United States. My brother moved into my condo when I left town, and our arrangement saved me a fortune in taxes. Traveling was very interesting but it kept me moving every three months, often hundreds of miles each time. I couldn't become a landlord under those conditions, but I periodically read books on the subject and the idea smoldered like an ember in the back of my brain.

I met my wife in Seattle while travel nursing, and after we married we moved to Tennessee for graduate school. I received my Master's of Science in Nursing and became a Certified Registered Nurse Anesthetist (CRNA) in early 2012.

In 2012 our family moved back to Oklahoma City to start the next chapter of our lives. Graduate school had drained our resources and were broke. So I looked into selling the condo for some much needed cash.

My condominium had fallen into disrepair and needed some work. Unfortunately, a large apartment complex just north of my condo went into bankruptcy and closed down while I was gone. Vandals frequently broke through the fence and set fires to this partially burned out relic from the 1970's. The eyesore killed area property values. I owed about $17,000.00 on my 30 year mortgage. The condo needed a few thousand dollars worth of work to get top dollar. Sadly, the best price we could hope for was only about $25,000.00. We stood to make about $5,000.00 before commissions and seller's concessions - like paying the buyer's closing costs. We may have been able to net a paltry three grand.

What a tremendous opportunity!

It was no secret to my spouse that I wanted to be a landlord, though she was lukewarm on the idea at best. I laid out the scenario carefully and let the money do the talking. The figures convinced her to let me rent the place instead of selling it. Plus, I reckoned if she saw how great it was to get a check in the mail every month for doing nothing, then maybe we could do this landlord thing for real!

After a little research, I found the condo could rent for $580.00/month. With overhead expenses of $200.00 for the mortgage and $100.00 in HOA fees, we would clear a tidy $280.00 every month. And more importantly, I would have established proof of concept.

We were broke. Neither of us had worked in three years, my paychecks were less than expected, grad school had wiped out our retirement accounts, and we had a lot of bills to pay. We decided that I should do the repairs to the condo myself and use the credit card.

I moved some tools into the condo and got to work.

Chapter 4: My First Mistake

Working on houses sucks.

Working on houses REALLY sucks when you have a full time job and a family at home. My brother moved out of the condo in August, and I wanted to rent it by September. I figured a few weekends and I would have the place whipped into shape. However, my wife wanted us to be a family (oh yeah, that...). We decided to eat breakfast together every day I wasn't at work, and I should be home in time for dinner. So, I dedicated every Sunday (from 9am-4pm) until I had the place ready to go.

Then I started finding problems. Every project seemed to create another project. Each repair took twice as long and cost twice as much as expected (even though I purposefully over estimated on both before I started). I spent hours in home improvement stores making mind numbing decisions before buying materials that I then had to install. September came and went, followed by October, November, and most of December. Did I mention we were pregnant? We had a baby early that December. Everything was challenging, and stressful.

We were exhausted. I saved nothing by doing the work myself and caused a great deal of marital strain in the process. I should have hired somebody.

Costs to repair the condo over the course of four months:

LOST RENT $580 x 4 = $2,320.00

MATERIALS: $3,000.00

CARRYING COSTS:

Mortgage payments: $200.00 x 4 = $800.00

HOA dues: $100.00 x 4 = $400.00

Utilities: $200.00 x 4 = $800.00

Total: $7,320.00. **Plus time I'll never get back**.

Why was I wasting my time doing $20.00/hour labor? I was killing my weekends and stressing everybody out, especially **myself**. I could have taken a cash advance on my credit card, paid someone $5,000.00 to do all the work, and had the place rented in September like I had originally planned.

When you tell other people you are planning on being a landlord, they are going to look at you like you're nuts. "I know this guy who did it and he was an angry man because he was fixing houses all the time." Or they'll say, "My dad had a bunch of rent houses and we spent every weekend painting them, and I hated it!" "Are you crazy?"

Don't let your properties run your life. Can I lay a tile floor? Yes. Do I find it an enjoyable pastime? No! I'd rather be on a boat.

I can't do as good a job as the guy from the flooring store can. I don't have all the specialty tools to lay tile, nor do I want them eating up space in my garage. I tiled the downstairs of that condo myself. I was sore, miserable, and dirty. The work took a very long time. Several Sundays were wasted. Another month of rent was gone, and I incurred carrying costs. No money was saved and, on top of all that, I hurt my finger.

Pay someone else to repair your properties. There are people out there who want to do this for a living. Trust me, it ain't you.

Wait! You said this book was about doing all this stuff without spending your own money! And now you're saying you spent a bunch on that condo!

I did. This book isn't about my condo. That experience was the beginning. I'm telling you this story so you don't make the same mistakes I did. That lesson cost me thousands, and I'm giving it to you (almost) for free. This book is about what happened next.

Chapter 5: Stumbling Across Experience

The condo got rented, and the checks started coming in. My phone didn't ring off the hook with the dreaded "water heater problem"* or anything else. We simply got paid.

*Why does everyone worry about getting calls in the middle of the night about a water heater? Nobody takes a shower then. I've heard more people who aren't landlords ask me how I deal with "getting called about a water heater," tenfold more than anything else. Those things last 10-15 years. They are a big can of water with a heating element inside. Yes, I've replaced water heaters. But I've replaced refrigerators and stoves more often and they are more expensive than a stupid water heater. Don't worry about water heaters. There are bigger problems in this world.

My wife reluctantly agreed with me that the whole landlord thing was working. I wanted to go bananas and get more places to rent. If one property could bring in $580.00, ten of them could get me $5,800.00 right? We could pay our student loan bills and have money left over. I found a solution to my debt problem! And once the debt got paid off, I would have a bunch of houses that generated income. I lost a lot of sleep mulling this over.

We met a guy at a carpet store when we were finishing up the condo. The carpet salesman was a landlord and steered us in the right direction with rental grade carpet. The salesman also gave us advice that changed our future. He told us about the Oklahoma City Real Estate Investor's Association. OKCREIA met the second Thursday of every month at a hotel not far from our house. My wife told me that if I was going to do the landlord thing, I needed to network. Networking went against my "me against the world" demeanor, but I knew she was right. In order to pull an idea of this magnitude off, I needed all the help I could get. I grudgingly agreed. I was willing to do whatever she wanted in order to get us out of financial hot water. We had six months before our loan payments came out of forbearance. I wasn't sure what the REIA club could do for me. Heck, I fixed that condo myself and got it rented to boot. I was already an expert.

To find your local REIA online, try searching for "[your state] REIA". The national REIA is found at nationalreia.org, but doesn't seem to include all state and local REIAs that exist. My local REIA is very active yet not listed.

That first REIA meeting changed the course of our lives. That night's REIA speaker was a guy named Russell. He started out young and with no money, now he had gobs of houses and some commercial real estate.

I had no idea what the lending environment had turned into. My experience with buying houses was dated. It had been a few years since I'd bought anything, and the only places I had bought up to that point were personal residences. I never put any money down before, I just signed forms and got the keys. So my plan was to do what I'd always done, walk up to a mortgage broker, use half an ink pen signing a stack of papers, and pick up a house. But those days are over, and you sure can't do that with rent houses anymore. The banks want you to have "skin in the game", also known as your own money. The crash of 2008 had the mortgage industry backed against the wall, and Fannie Mae won't let you get more than four mortgages without putting at least 40% down.

After talking about the brave new lending environment, Russell told us about the four rules of real estate:

1. Location

2. Location

3. Location

4. Buy it with someone else's money.

He told us to read Robert Allen's book, "Nothing Down for the 2000's"[1]. So I did.

That book was far more interesting to me than anything I read in grad school. Holy cow, the ideas were so simple, yet revolutionary! Yes, you have to use money to buy houses, but why in the world would you want to use your own? Houses are expensive. I read "Rich Dad, Poor Dad" by Robert Kiosaki[2]. My thoughts about debt had a major paradigm shift. I also read "Landlording on Auto-Pilot" by Mike Butler[3] (I've since read it several more times) and got tons of free documents and hundreds of great ideas from him.

It never occurred me to start asking people for money! You have to bone up, but you've done that before, right? This isn't mid-terms, this is over REAL MONEY. The motivation is self-propelled, powerful, and intoxicating. Once you start on the course becoming a real estate investor, you will become absolutely obsessed. It's an amazing experience and one hell of an adventure!

Every real estate book I read led to another. The education was effortless, bordering on compulsive. I couldn't shut up about it. THAT WAS THE KEY. REAL ESTATE IS A PERPETUAL MOTION MACHINE. I drew up a business plan, and I started pitching it to everyone. I had a solid plan replete with supporting, verifiable data. I wanted money so bad I couldn't stand it. There are lots of free business plan websites that give great instructions. Just search for "business plan" online.

I read a book on starting a Limited Liability Company, "NOLO's Quick LLC"[4] (easier than writing a business plan). Five minutes online and $125.00 later, I had my own company. The company's main goal? To use rental real estate to pay for my student loans, of course. WHAT A COUNTRY!

The plan was simple: Get as much money as I could from individuals, buy houses and get them rented. Once things were in motion, I would take the houses to the bank and get a loan against them collateral. Use the bank money to buy more houses. Then repeat as necessary.

While starting my little business, I kept thinking back to my first REIA meeting. Russell pointed out cheap houses have the highest return on investment, and given my situation this type of property appeared to fit the bill. I started combing real estate websites and Craigslist. Overwhelmed with data, I printed out a map of my city, plotted the asking rent at locations and overlaid them with the price for the house. While researching, I saw several Craigslist postings by a landlord who was moving out of state. The houses looked promising and were half what I was looking to pay, but commanded the same rent. One house was listed for $20,000.00 and rented for $600.00 per month, the other was $32,000.00 and rented for $750.00 per month. The only problem was, these homes were for sale in a part of town that *terrified* me. I called the selling landlord, who sounded like a "good ol' boy", and told him my situation. I explained I was interested in renting in Northwest Oklahoma City, but didn't see numbers like his from the East side of town. He told me, "Buddy, if you want to make money, the East side will get you a ton more than anywhere else in this city." He bid me good luck and our conversation ended. He wasn't going to wait until I had money to buy what he was offering, but this single interaction changed my focus.

East Oklahoma City is a low income area. Bars are on the windows of many shops and houses. There is a izeable number of vacant and/or boarded up houses. The population is primarily African American and pretty foreign to a white guy from the suburbs like me.

I nervously drove to the East side to see the houses in person. My eyes darted around looking for threats from all directions. It was hard to analyze the properties since all I really wanted to do was leave. I was scared because of personal events from several years ago. The flashbacks were so intense I should have counted my drive as a cardio workout.

Chapter 6: It Was a Dark and Stormy Night

I must digress for a little bit here. Pardon the change of pace, time and subject, but this story gives insight regarding my fear:

May 3, 1999 is a notorious date in Oklahoma. One of the deadliest F-5 tornado outbreaks in history happened that day. The worst casualties were in the Moore/Oklahoma City area but the tornadoes didn't stop there, the devastating storm system rolled Northeast spinning up multiple twisters along the way. A small town was completely wiped off the map as the maelstrom headed toward Tulsa...where I sat, drinking at a bar with a friend.

My good friend Cathy and I were hanging out that evening downing beers when the weather suddenly went to hell. The tornado outbreak was being covered on TV, and the worst part of the storm appeared to be on a course that would miss us. It was pouring outside so we decided to wait it out. Occasionally the door would swing open and a drenched person or two would run inside and find a seat. At one point, two seemingly out of place black men came in from the deluge and wandered around the bar looking for a place to sit. There were a couple of extra chairs at our table and we had a good view of the television. One of the guys asked if anyone else was sitting with us, we said no and invited them to sit down. The talkative one told us they were walking home and got caught in the storm. We called for a couple more glasses and shared the pitcher of beer. Our foursome exchanged small talk and watched the uninterrupted weather report on TV.

Then the storm changed direction. Another F-5 tornado dropped down close to town and the weatherman flipped out, screaming, "Run for cover, get underground, this thing is a killer! It's half a mile wide and heading straight for us!" As the meteorologist was yelling the tornado sirens spun up outside. Everyone in the bar looked around and a couple of people near the door ran outside. The bartender yelled, "This place doesn't stand a chance! Get out of here now! The f---ing bar is closed! GO!!!" Everyone headed for the door at the same time. Cathy and I were crammed together at the bottleneck caused by the rush of people at the door.

One of the men who had joined us grabbed my shoulder as we made it outside. He yelled, "We were just walking home and got caught in this storm! We won't make it before the tornado gets here! Can you please give us a ride? It's not very far by car!" Cathy heard him over the noise of the storm and sirens, she nodded yes and we covered our heads and splashed through the parking lot to her truck. From the back seat our passengers called out directions. Shortly after we started driving we had to stop in the middle of the road to let a dumpster blow across the street. The guy behind me asked to be let out, so I crammed my seat as far forward as I could and opened the door (The truck was a two door "sport" edition). He immediately disappeared into sheets of rain and blackness. We drove on, guided by our remaining passenger who said he was taking us to his cousin's house. The guy said, "Me and my cousin bought a bunch of beer today and I want to give you some. You were so nice and shared your beer with me and now you're saving my life." We declined, acknowledging that he was making a nice gesture, but we were in a hurry to get out of the way of the tornado. "Here's my cousin's house, pull over in the driveway. I'm not going to let you leave empty handed. I'm not usually in a place to pay somebody back, but today I can. Come on!"

Cathy had to get out to let him exit, the steering wheel wouldn't let her slide the seat forward far enough for him to squeeze out. She said, "Ok, fine, but we've got to get out of here." They ran to the porch so I got out and followed my friend.

It was very dark. We were in a bad part of town with no street lights during a massive storm. It was midnight on a Monday so the house lights were off too. However, the lightning was intense, so I could clearly see the gun pointed at me. Our new acquaintance's demeanor instantly changed. He identified himself as a gang member, snatched Cathy's car keys out of her hand, and told us we were being robbed. He snarled, "Gimme your wallet!"

I was completely furious and shouted, "F--- you man! You can't rob us right now! We just saved your life! Give her back her-."

He pistol whipped me in the face. I cannot describe to you how much that hurts. Everything went white for an instant as waves of pain reverberated through my head. I opened my eyes when the gold chain around my neck was yanked off and was surprised to find myself standing. Yelling, I shoved him hard and he fell off the porch.

Not clearly thinking, I jumped after him.

The alcohol in my system got an adrenaline boost causing me to misjudge my jump. We crashed foreheads together, then began grappling at each other. I felt cold metal on the back of my neck and realized he was still holding his gun. A sense of doom came over me as the gravity of my situation became clearer (This is the first fight I had ever been in, and it probably wasn't going to end well). I got my arms between us and shoved him backwards again. A bright light and loud noise emanated from his right hand. My right thigh felt as though someone had put a lit cigarette on it and a powerful sensation of heat traveled through my leg. I had that sinking feeling you get at the base of your spine when suddenly there's a cop in your rear view mirror and you realize you are speeding. I tried to brush the "heat" off my thigh despite the fact that I was soaked and standing in a torrential downpour. The gang member leveled his pistol at my face and rolled the hammer back with his thumb. My life flashed before my eyes as I stared down the barrel of an unmistakably functional firearm. It seemed like a long time before he spoke.

"I said, give me your wallet!"

So I did! I slowly pulled my wallet out of my pocket, then threw it at his face to get the gun out of mine. My assailant caught the wallet, then pivoted towards Cathy's truck. The sound of her car alarm being disabled snapped my friend out of the catatonic state she'd entered at the sight of the pistol.

Cathy ran toward her truck, but I was between them. I grabbed her and her momentum spun us in the yard as the truck started up. She cried, "Oh my God Mike! He's stealing my car!" We were lit by her tail-lights as I replied, "Let him go, I think he shot me!"

The squealing of tires drowned out the wailing of storm sirens as we instinctively ran away from the vehicle. Half a block of flooded street later we found ourselves at an intersection. I started moving toward a house that had its lights on, the front door open, and a bunch of children sitting on the porch steps. Cathy grabbed my arm and said, "What are you doing?"

"I'm going to that house! My leg hurts, something is wrong!"

She was hysterical, "What if those are the people who just robbed us and shot you?"

I shouted, "Then we'll go to another house!"

"That's a stupid plan!"

The wide eyed children on the porch parted for me to pass as I charged into their house. Finally in the light, I looked down and saw a small hole in my blood soaked jeans, and promptly...lost it. "Auuuugh! I've been shot!"

The man of the house was standing in front of me wearing only sweat pants. A foot taller than myself and covered in muscles, he quizzically watched while I frantically unfastened my jeans and dropped them to the floor. I saw a bleeding hole in the front of my thigh and began blubbering and pacing in a circle, my strides limited by how far my jeans would allow my ankles to go. Eventually, I spiraled to the floor where I could see water pouring into the living room through a large crack in the ceiling. The children gathered around and stared. Cathy (who had borrowed the man's phone) finished cussing out the 911 operator and returned to the living room where she explained our situation to our unwitting host.

Seeking clarification he asked, "They said they was Crips?"

"Yes." She replied.

He looked at me and said, "And you tried to fight 'em?"

"Yes." I muttered.

He shook his head, "You lucky to be alive. Them boys don't mess around."

"No kidding." I sheepishly agreed. The vision of angry eyes staring over the barrel of a gun constantly looped in my mind while I cradled my leg.

Cathy interrupted, "Someone's coming!" Our big friend walked over to the front door and peered up the street. Then he shouted, "They are coming back, this is a drive by!" He slapped light switches and the house went dark. He yelled, "Everybody get down on the floor!" and dove to the ground grabbing his smallest children. The big guy wrapped himself around the toddlers with his back to the wall. I stared out the open door toward the street, completely paralyzed with fear. For the second time in 20 minutes I was certain I was about to die. My heart beat furiously as I tried not to move, sobbing children were laying all around me and their father was telling everyone to be quiet. An old Cadillac slowly came into view, its headlights off as it ground almost to a stop in front of the house. I kept hoping to wake up, as surely this was a nightmare.

The Cadillac pulled into the driveway across the street and two people got out, running. My heart was already at its maximum rate, so I'm pretty sure it simply stopped. The people from the car turned and ran into the house they had pulled up to. I don't know why their headlights were off. Maybe they were burned out and these neighbors were driving slowly because they couldn't see. After a few seconds I gave the all clear from my spot on the floor. Everyone got up but me. I couldn't take any more, so I laid on the floor with my pants half off. At some point the tornado sirens wound down.

The police showed up a little later, guns drawn and pointed at Big Guy. Cathy threw herself in front of the cops and screamed at them to leave him alone.

Everything got sorted out at 120 decibels and the police holstered their firearms. The paramedics were next to arrive. As they struggled to get their gurney out of the truck in the rain I sat up and told the cops, "I can walk!" I pulled up my pants and climbed into the ambulance, safe at last. "Get me the hell out of here!"

The paramedic stripped off my clothes (standard practice if someone's been shot, victims don't always notice multiple injuries). He grabbed his walkie-talkie and announced to the receiving Emergency Room, "Entry and exit wound to right thigh." I rotated my leg and looked at the side of my thigh, the hole there was larger than the one in front and some tissue was dangling freely (the hole was smaller than a nickel, but I didn't know it existed until then). Over the noise of the ambulance and storm, I'm pretty sure anyone outside the truck would have heard me shout, "I HAVE AN EXIT WOUND!!!"

The police confiscated my jeans and boxer shorts as evidence. I was 105 miles from home without any clothing from the waist down. Traumatized and intoxicated, we couldn't describe our assailants with any degree of accuracy. My wallet was found inside Cathy's purse in a grocery bag at the side of the road. Her (brand new) truck was found a couple of days later, missing its battery, the CD changer (a big deal in 1999), her stethoscope and some Mardi Gras beads. Someone tried to pry the stereo out of her truck, then gave up after tearing up the dashboard. No one ever got caught, and the Tulsa Police still have my pants.

34

I'm sure this event caused me PTSD, though I never sought treatment. Buying houses in a neighborhood just like the one I was shot in has been unnerving at times. Working the low income area has been an immersion therapy for me. I'm not scared anymore, but I was a bundle of nerves at first. Now I chuckle when people tell me I'm going to get shot and I get to tell them it's too late. Having such a vivid near death experience has made me stronger; I appreciate life more because of what I went through. Also, I have a good barometer for what a "bad day" is. When my little world blows up around me I start laughing about it. "At least I'm not about to get shot in the face by an angry gang member and left to die with a tornado bearing down on me today." Things could be worse.

Chapter 7: These Real Estate Books Work!

Enough back story, let's return to 2013.

I had a company and a business plan, all I lacked was tens of thousands of dollars to make it work. After unsuccessfully pitching the plan to an acquaintance, I called my mother to ask her for a phone number of a wealthy person we both knew. She said, "I don't know if Phil will go for that idea, but I'll see what I can do." The next day she called me back, "I've crunched some numbers, and I can get a loan against my 401k. I was also about to restructure my home equity line of credit, and can probably get some more out of that if you need it." I was dumbfounded. Borrowing cash from my mother was not something I had even considered, but she liked my plan, saw my level of dedication, and knew I had the determination to pull everything off. A few days later, my cousin met mom and my family for breakfast. He asked what was new, so I told him about my new venture. After discussing things for a little while he said, "I want in." My cousin had some extra money and banks weren't paying even one percent interest, so I offered to pay him five percent in an amortized note over the next five years. He liked the idea, and we drew up a financial agreement. Between the two parties I suddenly found myself with $70,000.00 to invest. Holy crap, the advice written in these real estate books actually WORKS!

I used to think having $1,000.00 wagered on a single roll of the dice was gambling. But real estate took the game to another level. I was now gambling with more money than most people earn in a year and failure meant going down in flames. The good news was real estate turns you into the "house". In other words, you can become the casino with all the odds in your favor. No more sucker bets for me.

A couple of weeks after striking deals with my family I had checks in hand. I was very nervous standing in line at the bank. Sure, over the years I'd had several hundred thousand dollars go in and out of bank accounts. But this was the first time I had so much money on me. I rehearsed what I was going to say and had several forms of identification ready. I didn't want the teller to get suspicious, thinking I was a drug dealer or something. How many people were going to scrutinize my deposit? How long was I going to have to wait there? Were they going to put me in an office and start making phone calls?

No.

The cashier hardly looked up. She typed a couple of numbers into her computer, handed me a receipt, and wished me a nice day. Then she cocked her eyebrow. I was dumbfounded! I realized I was frozen in place staring at the receipt so I managed to stammer out, "Umm... OK... You have a nice day too." There were people waiting behind me. I snapped out of it and ran out of the bank like Forrest Gump. "Woo hoo! I'm a real estate investor!"

The pressure to get the money working was intense. I didn't want to waste any of the borrowed funds making payments back to my lenders. I wanted a house as soon as possible. Unfortunately, the deal I previously found on Craigslist was long gone. There were no other offers online by any other landlords selling occupied properties once I had my funding secured. I checked out some other listings that were "handyman specials." The first few houses I went to were all but destroyed. No one bothered to meet me at their properties on my first couple of outings. The property owners simply told me to go to their house and look around. I crawled through broken windows using cinder blocks as steps, or simply walked into the house from the back because the rear wall was missing. Daylight was visible through multiple holes in the ceilings and roofs and I stepped carefully past open holes into crawl spaces. I was afraid of running across squatters or whatever else my imagination could come up with. But nobody wanted to squat in places like these.

Then I found a better looking house on Craigslist. It was a two bed, one bath, 1000 square foot home on a quarter acre lot that would easily rent for $550.00 per month. It definitely needed work but it was in the best shape I'd seen so far. The guy wanted $18,000.00. I got him down to $17,000.00, but I had to act fast, he had this other investor that was interested...

Chapter 8: Caveat Emptor

Yes, you can buy houses off Craigslist. I buy a lot of stuff from Craigslist. I'm sitting on my Craigslist chair with my feet on my Craigslist ottoman, watching my Craigslist TV, right next to my Craigslist dog while writing this. My wife is next to me on our Craigslist couch, possibly looking at Craigslist.

Don't buy your first house off Craigslist! Sure, you can use the site to purchase real estate, but don't do it until you *REALLY* know what a good deal is. Buy a few houses through a realtor first. Shady investors sell houses on Craigslist, many of whom couldn't sell their house by traditional means because their property is worthless.

My guy called me an "investor", told me he was "wholesaling" the house. He used buzzwords I had recently learned from my real estate books. I brought up some concerns about the house.

"Why is the ceiling falling in?"

"Oh, it's just an old house, plaster loses its grip after a while. All you gotta do is put some quarter inch Sheetrock up there. It will cover up those holes and keep the rest from falling down."

Okay, that's reasonable.

"Why isn't there an electric meter on the base beside the breaker box?"

"Well, this place has been empty for quite some time. The electric company pulls their meters so nobody takes them. All you gotta do is call and they'll put another one back on. You'll be good to go."

The breaker box was full of circuit breakers. The house had outlets, light fixtures and light switches. A new meter seemed tenable.

"I don't know man. I don't have any guys to do work like this..."

"Guys? I got guys coming out of my ears who want to work with an investor like you! We get this deal put together and I'll get you some guys that do good, affordable work fast! I just got off the phone with someone wanting work."

"Can I get his number? I'd like to see what he thinks about this place."

"Shi-! I ain't giving my contacts to you! This house is a good deal and you know it. You already got me down to 17 grand, I'm bleeding to death over here and you're trying to scam me on this deal. You put a-couple-a thousand into this place, get it rented and it will buy itself in two years."

"Does the plumbing work? There's a padlock on the shut off valve and the city pulled the meter so we can't check it..."

"Of course it works. People steal water in this part of town. Same with the electricity, just call the water company and you're good to go. Now, I thought you were an investor. I can't spend all day with you wasting my time. I got a guy coming up from Dallas tomorrow who's gonna buy this place if you don't."

I actually cut this guy a check for $3,000.00. We were to close in 2 weeks. A freaking house for $17,000.00, are you kidding me?

A block past the house I had a pain in my gut, a serious case of buyer's remorse. When I got home my wife could tell something was wrong. I told her that I didn't want to go through with the deal.

"What??? You want to throw away three thousand dollars! Are you crazy? Absolutely not! You said this was a good house and we were going to make all this money off it, and now it changed?"

Our four year old was staring at me, the baby was crying. I went through with it. I consider this purchase to be the price of my GED in real estate investment. I'll tell you what I learned next. You're welcome.

Chapter 9: You're Gonna Get Shot!

Plenty of people have told me, "You're gonna get shot.", after I described the area of town which I held rental properties. Obviously, the thought crossed my mind. But I had too much at risk to let stress turn me back. Besides, I decided landlording was going to fix my student loan problem one way or another. I was either going to become a successful landlord or die trying. Student loans get erased if you pass away before you pay them off. If you get wiped out, your loans do too!*

Death is one of only three options to wipe out your loan debt, and if someone like your parents co-signed and they are still alive...well, it's not really your problem anymore, now is it? I'm not advocating Hari Kari. The purpose of this note is to inform you that you can't even get away from student loan debt by declaring bankruptcy. The three ways to get out of federal student loan debt are (in order of most to least desirable): 1.) Pay them off, in full, as fast as you can. 2.) Participate in a repayment plan and fulfill your obligations. 3.) Die.

Do I carry a gun?

No.

I've owned guns and have fired thousands of rounds throughout my life. I was shot in Tulsa because

I tried to fight an armed robber. I learned my lesson and have a new plan: If someone points a pistol at me and demands my wallet... I will give it to them. I carry less money than the pizza guy. A mugger can have my truck too; it's insured. The only scenario where I see myself at gunpoint is if someone tries to rob me, and I don't want to introduce another weapon into that equation. If I'd had a gun the night I was shot I probably would have been hurt far worse, likely killed. Think about it. If someone is going to rob you, do they warn you first? Hell no! The gun will be in your face. If you try and pull one out, your assailant will have a limited number of options and a significant advantage. Let's say you somehow manage to get the upper hand and blast the bad guy to bits. Then what? You just **killed** somebody. You can still go to jail, you can get sued by the surviving family, or you can get shot from across the street by a fellow gang banger who was watching from the shadows. I don't look for trouble, so it usually doesn't find me. If I got robbed and they took everything on my person, I would walk to one of my rentals, borrow a tenant's phone, call the cops, and then call my wife for a ride home. Everyone stays alive. More than 90 people die every day in this country because of gun violence. I don't want to add to that number, especially as a statistic.

For safety reasons, I tell my tenants to mail their rent to my PO Box. First of all, I'm not wasting my time driving around town each month collecting cash rent or getting to hear excuses in person. When tenants request personal rent collection, I won't do it. I ask them, "Do you really want to advertise you likely have $600.00 cash on you the first of every month? I'm not going to drive the money train down the block. I've been shot before and I don't want it to happen again." The wheels turn, eyes dart around, and they buy stamps.

Safety hasn't been an issue since I started doing this. Nothing has been stolen, and nobody working on any of my houses has been robbed. I don't anticipate any future problems either. Yes, people get shot and killed close to my rentals. They get shot near my primary residence as well. I don't get shot because I'm asleep at 2:00 a.m. I'm not drunk at a party that has gotten out of hand. Nor am I out buying heroin, smacking my spouse around, or trying to rob someone. I'm at my rentals in the daytime, and I spend the least amount of time at them as I possibly can. I have other things to do, and I didn't buy houses so I could hang out at them. I bought them so I wouldn't have to work as hard, or as much, to make a few (thousand) bucks.

Chapter 10: This House Needs a Priest, Not a Contractor

The first house I bought with borrowed money was a mistake. I was blinded by the deal, the price, my enthusiasm, and the false pressure from a scam artist. There was no "other investor" about to snag the place out from under me. Nobody wanted the place. Knowing what I do now, I wouldn't have taken the house if it was given to me for **FREE**.

Lesson 1: Lights Need Wires.

The first order of business was to get the power on, so I called the electric company.   They informed me that they couldn't help. In order to get another meter, my dump had to pass a meter base inspection by the city. It took a little research, but I found the number and then called the electrical inspector's office and got ahold of the scheduler. I told them I had a full time job and could meet the inspector on Saturday. They said they would put me in for an inspection on Saturday morning, but would prefer Friday late afternoon. My schedule was tight that Friday.   I asked, "Please have them call me before they leave so we can verify I can get there." Apparently, city inspectors don't like waiting. No follow up call came, I got stuck at work late on Friday, and my phone rang at 2:30 p.m. The guy was MAD that no one was there to meet him. He told me I failed the inspection first because he had no access to the property. I said, "There's a lockbox on the door and the combination is-". He gruffly interrupted, "I don't even need to go inside, do you know how old that breaker box is? There's a large gap between the cover and breakers, if someone reached in there it would kill them. Call an electrician."

The electrician quoted me $750.00 to install a new breaker box. I was hoping to put $3,000.00 max into the place. Installing this metal box meant 25% of my budget was already spent. But nobody wants to live in a house without electricity, so I cut a check to the electrician.

The electrician did a nice job. Moved a large, modern breaker box inside, then he called me, "I have bad news." "OK." I said and hoped it somehow was a small thing. Then he matter of factly told me my house didn't have any wires.

"What?!?"

"Somebody stole all the wiring out of this house and sold it for scrap. All that's left up here is some old knob and tube, and they cut that before giving up. We have to start over."

Bye-bye budget. It costs around $6,000.00 to re-wire a 1000 square foot house to code. I know this because I had a few quotes. I really know this because paying that much money stings. I have a scar on my wallet to this day.

If you are considering buying your first rent house without an inspection, flip all the light switches and check the outlets. Walk away if there is no power. If the person selling the house has the power off to "save money", assume they are lying to you. Tell them you have to assume the house needs a complete re-wire, and drop your offer accordingly. The deal will fall apart, and they will look for another sucker. Don't start off with a $6K mistake.

Lesson 2: Avoid "Bad Luck."

Once we got the lights on, I could better see the condition of the house (several windows were boarded up). It was riddled with bullet holes! Apparently, someone had made their last stand in the bathroom. A litter of kittens were starting their lives off in the laundry room and it smelled accordingly. The holes in the ceilings and floors looked a lot larger. The foundation was broken.

My phone calls to the guy that sold me the house, of course, went unanswered. His platoon of "guys" must have all found too much work.

I called a contractor and told him I wanted the house fixed and my budget was $5,000.00. Once he stopped laughing he said, "Buddy, you have at least $10,000.00 worth of work here, and that's if I don't find anything else wrong."

I found a painter/remodeler on Craigslist. He looked the part, covered in paint, and drove a pickup truck. I made the assumption he knew what he was doing. He quoted a reasonable price to do some work saying, "Oh, yeah, we can get this done for five grand, prolly less," so off we went. Don't take on someone who needs a check every day. It's exhausting. "I need a check for $37.00 to buy some paint." "I told some guy to come over and fix that window, but he never showed up. We have bad luck." I wanted to pay him in advance one week because I was going to be busy. I couldn't break away to pay him $60.00 so he could buy screws and wood one day, then $80.00 for labor the next day etc. Without money this guy would quit working - he couldn't afford the materials. He protested, "I need to have that money in front of me, it gives me fire." I insisted and explained my situation. He hesitantly took the money. Then he took another job. A week later I called him and asked, "Why isn't the drywall fixed yet?"

"Mr. Mike, we had some bad luck. I had this guy lined up to help me, then he bailed. I had to do some other work to pay my rent. It will only take a couple of days."

Your handy man should have a good grasp of the scope of work, give an estimate, and be able to afford to eat while doing your job. Sure you can provide materials up front (if you trust someone), but you don't want to have to pay someone every single day. It's obnoxious, and there are better guys out there. If your guy turns into one of these, get someone else. Make them someone else's bad luck.

Always pay handymen AFTER the work is done. Pay them quickly, so they will drop someone else's job to come do yours.

When the handyman finally got back to my job it was raining…inside.

Lesson 3: Three Layers of Shingles are not Better than One.

The house had a roof, the shingles were a couple of different colors, but none were missing (that I could tell). One layer of shingles is what houses start off with. If the shingles get damaged, you can tear off the roof and put on another or overlay the shingles with a second set. Obviously, an overlay involves less labor and is cheaper than a tear off and re-shingle. A reasonable roofer would never lay a third layer of shingles, they are too heavy, and decking (the wood underneath) cannot properly support that much weight. My house picked up a third layer somewhere along the way. The shingles, decking and a few rafters were shot. We had to do a complete tear off and re-decking to the tune of another $6,000.00.

My handyman was off on another "quick job" and didn't seem interested in finishing my house. I called the previous contractor who was then professional enough to leave out an, "I told you so." Work had been painfully slow, and I needed to rent the place as quickly as possible.

To make a long story short, the contractor cost me another $12,000.00. My house didn't look haunted anymore but still had no heat or air conditioning.

I saw window A/C units with heat at the store. Sweet! I didn't know they even made things like that. Problem solved and they were modular. The house didn't have to rely on a single heat and air system that could break down. If one unit broke I would only be out the $400.00 it cost. I needed one for each room so there went another $1,600.00.

Carpet installed for $1,300.00 finished the remodel. Three long months of bringing this house back from the grave made it habitable again. We moved tenants in immediately.

Electric:	$6,000.00
Roof:	$6,000.00
"Handy man":	$3,000.00
Contractor:	$12,000.00
Climate Control (part one):	$1,600.00
Carpet:	$1,300.00

Total spent on repairs: $29,000.00. Add my purchase price and I had a $46,000.00 house in a $25,000.00 neighborhood.

Lesson 4: Tenants Find Problems Contractors Miss.

Fortunately, the water worked once we got a meter reinstalled, but the new shower didn't drain after 10 minutes of running. The kitchen sink drain leaked into the cabinet after washing a few dishes. Tree roots had grown into the sewer line. A thousand bucks here, a couple of thousand there, and I was now $50,000.00 into this property. Then winter came. The A/C with heat units were installed in the summer. If you put your hand in front of the vent in July and turned on "Heat", it was like a hair dryer on high. But in December, the puny 580 watts of heat they put out could only turn a freezing room into a slightly less freezing room. I bought space heaters. The house had a floor furnace that had been underwater because of the sewer line, and the wall heater was no longer functional and was so old repair parts were not available. Also, the gas system would not hold pressure, hence our all electric conversion during the re-wire. My tenants were cold and not pleased. I insulated the attic, but the old, single pane windows were very drafty.

The final solution for climate control at this house was to install Packaged Terminal Air Conditioners (PTAC). PTACs are the things you find under the windows in a hotel room, they can both heat and cool a place. It costs a fair bit of money to put them in. A big hole has to be cut in the wall for their mounting sleeve, and the electrical has to be upgraded to handle the load. But these systems are often cheaper than putting in central heat and air. Each unit cost me $2,000.00 and it took three of them to cover the house's needs. My handyman charged me $1,000.00 to frame out the openings and install them, and my electrician had to come out and wire in outlets for them at $250.00 apiece. That upgrade cost me another $7,750.00.

Please don't let this chapter scare you out of real estate. If I'd used a realtor and/or had an inspection, then I would have gotten a far better deal. I was regularly going to REIA meetings while this disaster unfolded and got a lot of comfort from fellow investors. My peers told me they all bought a house they shouldn't have at some point. It simply comes with the territory. You learn A LOT. Don't expect to make a sweet deal the first time you buy a rental. You aren't out to steal a house, just to get an honest deal that will make you money and quickly. Despite this first deal, I still do my own inspections because I now know what I'm looking for. I buy houses with cash, so there is no bank to insist on an inspection. Also, a home inspection costs $300 and takes time to carry out. Getting an inspection is not going to change a deal that is listed "As-is."

I still own the place, though I had no business rehabilitating a property. I should have found a place that was ready to go. Preferably already rented to someone who wanted to stay. I shouldn't have convinced myself this house was the best deal I could find. Common sense went out the window and took a big chunk of change with it. Please don't buy your first house off Craigslist. Get some free help. Get a realtor.

Chapter 11: Use a Realtor

I told my stepsister's husband about my first "deal" before it closed. I didn't know him very well, but knew he was a real estate agent. What I didn't know cost me a ton of money. He was also a landlord, worked with investors that bought similar houses to mine, and had also been a builder. My brother-in-law was a compendium of knowledge. He took me under his wing.

The Multiple Listing System (MLS) is where almost every house in the United States is listed for sale. Realtors have the exclusive right to use the MLS; having access to every property for sale in your city is extremely beneficial. Your realtor can set up a search using parameters you set. Tell them the geographic area you want (bordered by streets), how much you want to spend (increase it a little above your budget - you may be able to haggle), and the type of property you are looking for. You will get an email that links to every for sale property in your area and price range. Plenty of landlords sell their properties through realtors.

Some of your listings will show notes like, "Already rented for $550 per month, tenant wants to stay." It's pretty easy to figure out that deal. I've bought houses like this before and frankly, I prefer this scenario over any other. Instant income is great!

Why would a landlord want to sell a house? I worried about that at first. If this place is making money, why get rid of it? There are lots of answers. Landlords move, they get old, the house bought itself four times and they are moving up, they could use an extra $35,000.00, the tenants are a nightmare, the spouse wasn't fully in on the idea and has an ultimatum, things need repairs, the landlord died and the family is splitting the estate, etc. Just because someone is selling something doesn't make it a bad deal. If you buy an occupied property you will probably meet the tenant at the showing. If you don't see them, get their number and call them. A tenant will tell you if anything is wrong with the house, and you can gauge if they are someone you want to deal with before you close. Your prospective tenant will be nervous. They probably like their house and their arrangement. I try to come off as approachable, but not a pushover. I read somewhere that people find strangers in a red shirt intimidating and those in a green shirt friendly, so I wear gray to keep things neutral.

My brother-in-law put together an MLS search, and a week later I saw a place I liked. It was a 2 bed / 1 bath / 1 car garage (2/1/1) brick house listed for $24,000.00. Brick houses are nice because they stop bullets; there were no holes in this one! You also never have to paint brick, and it never gets hail damage. I now exclusively buy brick houses. This house was dark inside, until I turned on the functioning (yeah!) lights. The curtains and carpet were about 50 years old, and the floor was warped in one spot. It only had two bedrooms, but the back of the house had a "party room", complete with a wet bar. There were no laundry hookups, but I came up with the idea to take out the bar, put in a stackable washer / dryer hookup and convert the remainder of the bar into a closet, making the back room a third bedroom and the house more marketable as a rental. We made an offer for $20,000.00, and the owners took it. The house was part of an estate with beneficiaries who lived across the country. It only cost a few thousand and a couple of weeks to repair this property. It's been rented for $650.00 per month ever since. That comes out to $7,800.00 per year from a $25,000.00 investment.

Buyers don't pay realtors, sellers do. Real estate agents get a 6% commission (split between them if there are two realtors on the deal) off the sale price, therefore, the seller receives that much less at closing. This arrangement means your realtor is always on the seller's side. The more a real estate agent can get you to agree to pay, the higher the commission they receive.

You have to search for a realtor who is willing to work with an investor. Any realtor would rather be selling a nice $300,000.00 house than some $30,000.00 junker. Think of the difference in commission: $18,000.00 vs $1,800.00 and it takes the *same amount of time* to close either deal. Consider yourself very lucky when you find someone who will work with you. So don't waste their time.

When I'm ready to buy, I check my MLS listings daily. The automatic search will send you an email every time a listing hits the market that matches your criteria. If something looks good, I drive by it as soon as possible. If I still like the place after I see it, I call my realtor immediately. This approach keeps me from booking unnecessary viewings of a place and being a nuisance.

Your first MLS search should provide you with several houses to choose from. Look yours over and realize that the listings often try to showcase the properties in the best light possible. If something has been on the market forever, *you don't want it either*. Don't even bother, and don't try to talk yourself into some deal that hundreds of people have passed up. A good deal only lasts a few days. Of course, in the beginning, check a few houses out on your list. Knowing what is out there at your price point is valuable, and seeing a few houses really helps highlight a decent buy when you find it. You may even be surprised, or get lucky. Some initial viewings will help your realtor better understand what you are looking for.

My realtor is usually booked up with appointments on the weekend, so I try and get some time off work on business days when I'm ready to buy. My realtor's schedule is more open on Tuesday morning than Saturday afternoon, and he'd like to spend some time with his family. Or at least his golf clubs.

Realtors have dedicated their career to buying and selling houses and they have tons of contacts. They know the local market and have experience dealing with people from all walks of life. There is simply no way a beginner to the world of landlording will be better connected and as knowledgeable as a professional in the field. Use a Realtor!

Chapter 12: The Banks These Days

Our company emerged from 2013 financially stricken. The money we raised should have been enough for three houses, but we were barely able to buy two. On the bright side, the education I gained was valuable (at least it cost a lot), and we had two houses rented and paying the bills. The private money we borrowed would take at least five years to pay back - not too bad considering a conventional mortgage takes 30 years. We were out of cash and needed a bank in order to expand further.

If you are a small time landlord, use a small bank. A quick way to determine if a bank is small is in its name. Small banks have the name of your state or city in their title. The big banks have set parameters to follow for lending, and a newbie might not fit their scheme.

Put together a financial statement before you meet your banker, you will have to generate one soon anyway. A personal financial statement is not a big deal to create, there are plenty of free forms online. The gist of a financial statement is to determine your net worth. Using grade school math, add up your assets, subtract your liabilities, and the result is your net worth. There are many free websites that will help you create a financial statement, simply search for "personal financial statement."

To find your assets, take all the big ticket items you own and calculate their values (Kelly Blue Book for car, Zillow for house). Then add that number to the cash you have in the bank and other accounts (like retirement, annuities, and whole life insurance).

To calculate your liabilities, add up the remaining balances on what you owe. Find the payoff on your car payments, mortgages, credit cards, and student loans. The sum of your debts are your total liabilities. Banks like people who have a positive net worth. But if you recently graduated college and are reading this book to pay off student loans, then you are probably "in the hole" just like I was. Here's where your local banker comes in handy. The lending officer at a big bank has to follow net worth guidelines and may not even talk to you. A local banker wants to keep their business in the community and is interested in developing a long term commitment with local businesses. Your local chief lending officer often has more latitude to make a loan than a large corporate banker. She may have only one person to answer to, or need a few more loans to fill her books.

I asked around my REIA group for ideas of where to start with a bank. Steven VanCauwenbergh "The Savvy Landlord" and I had talked a few times before and he shared a contact with me. I called the local banker and she was excited to talk to me, especially after she found out who gave me her number. The bank wanted to work with more investors, and I was rubbing elbows with successful ones. We set up a meeting for the next week, and I showed up early.

We chatted a little while, then got down to the financials.

She puzzled over my assets and liabilities, "Mike, you have no net worth!!"

I suddenly turned into Rodney Dangerfield.

"Tell me about it, I'm married and I got kids! ...That's not a problem is it?"

Her head bobbed from side to side, "Well, no, not necessarily."

She saw that my (very) negative net worth was due to student loan debt, but also acknowledged that my education had gotten me a lucrative job. What pushed her past saying no was that I was making it work. I had networked, knew the market, had a specific plan, and had proven the ability to get money when needed. I also had excellent credit, so she overlooked a few hundred thousand of debt.

I told the banker I wanted to mortgage my properties so I could free up cash to buy some more. She said, "It doesn't work that way anymore."

Mortgages on rent houses are harder to come by now. The crash of 2008 changed the lending environment. In order to hold a mortgage on a rental, you have to have a lot of money tied up in the property (a lot of skin in the game). Nowadays, a newcomer can only get a mortgage for around 75% of the assessed value of an investment property, and that's only if you have less than four mortgages. That way, if you default, the bank doesn't lose money. Once the bank forecloses on you they can sell your house and recoup their losses. Mortgaging my properties in an investor heavy area would have been an expansion limiting decision. I bought my second house cheap, but it wasn't assessed for much more than my purchase price. I bought the house for $20,000.00 and put about $5,000.00 into it, but it assessed for only $22,000.00 (Because the neighborhood was full of foreclosures and investment properties). The most I could have cashed out in a mortgage for that property would have been $16,500.00, and I couldn't do much with that. Besides, my banker wasn't even entertaining the idea. Instead, she offered me a line of credit for my properties. We had appraisals done on the two houses and the condominium, and she issued me a $100,000.00 line of credit using all three properties as collateral. I was to pay off my mortgage on the condo with the credit line, and the rest would be available for investments and improvements. What was even more awesome was the flexibility of a line of credit. The minimum payment each month was for the interest alone. And in 2014, we locked at 4.5%, or a little over $450.00 per month (if you maxed the credit line. If you only drew out half, the payment would be about $225.00 for $50,000.00). I gladly accepted the following terms:

The loan resets every year (allowing the bank to pump up the interest rates if they rise).

I was guaranteeing the credit line, so if I defaulted on a payment, then they could take all my houses, sell them, and I would still be liable to the bank for any left-over debt (in case the sale of my assets didn't cover the full amount). Another kicker about credit lines is the bank's ability to seize your assets much faster than through a mortgage foreclosure.

The credit line was a win-win to me! I wasn't going anywhere and the credit line allowed for quick expansion of my empire. All I had to do was send an email and I could head to the bank that afternoon to draw out whatever I needed. I could have a cashier's check in a matter of hours, and this allowed me to make a quick "cash offer," thereby removing the hassle of getting a mortgage along with buying a property.

Lines of credit are flexible, you can pay only the minimum (interest only) payment as you need, or pay them off at any time without penalty. If you pay back some of your credit line, and need to draw it out again, the bank will allow it at a moment's notice. You can write off the interest payments on a credit line just like a mortgage. A business line of credit does not impact the business owner's personal credit score. I was guaranteeing the credit line, but as long as my business pays its own bills, the line of credit does not show up when I make any other large purchases.

I have found utilizing a line of credit at a local bank to be a powerful tool. The ability to make a quick cash offer is a versatile way to expand a burgeoning real estate empire. Also, the flexibility of repaying any amount ranging from interest only to paying the credit line in full can suit your business whether times are bad or good.

Chapter 13: No Pay, No Stay

So far I've had to get rid of a few tenants for non-payment of rent. I try to work with people, but once someone gets too far down the hole, you have to either forgive their debt or get them to leave. I'm trying to run a business and I need rental income to make things work. My tenants and I have a long talk when we sign a lease. I explain that communication is the key to things working out well between us. Even if it is bad news, it needs to be communicated as soon as possible so we can formulate a plan.   If I don't get the rent and can't reach someone, then I have to start making assumptions and take action. The sooner, the better. The eviction process takes a few weeks, and every day that goes by without receiving rent hurts the bottom line. I need to keep my homes as profitable as possible, maintaining paying tenants, and weeding out those who have excuses instead of money orders. I try to head off the legal process by paying my deadbeat tenants cash to leave. The theory is you will get your place back faster, and in better condition, than if you use the authorities to get rid of someone.

My first foray into eviction happened with the condo. Payments had been getting later and shorter with un-kept promises of catching up. The first time I posted notice my tenant called and threw a fit, then paid (yay!).   A few months later, we were back in the same place, late and short. I made a generous offer to wipe out two months of late charges (ain't I a nice guy?) if she would catch up by a certain date. I had no response, so I posted notice. This time, however, she didn't call. So I sent an ultimatum by text message, "Pay me everything you owe by June 1st, including June's rent, or move out by the first and I will pay you $200.00 cash. If you don't do either of these I will be forced to evict you." They had 11 days to comply. She immediately got back in touch with me and said she was going to pay May 24th. I checked my phone frequently and sent text messages throughout the 24th with no response. I got angry. I unprofessionally texted her the next day, "I knew you were lying to me, now you need to move out by the first of June and get $200, or I will evict you." I got a court date for June 4th. All further attempts to contact them went unanswered. So I drove to the condo June 1st to post the court notice. This posting was not entirely necessary, but I was wondering what was going on at my property. The place appeared empty so I knocked on the door out of curiosity. No response. I was getting some tape out of my truck when the boyfriend opened the front door. Surprised, I half yelled, "Why are you still here? I was going to pay you cash to be gone by last night!" My tenant's boyfriend, "Calvin" who bore resemblance to Snoop Dogg, appeared intoxicated. "Look man, no man calls no other man's woman a liar." (I'm paraphrasing here, it took him a little while to actually mutter this to me.) I didn't go to my property to pick a fight. I knew Calvin had a gun, I had seen it laying out a few months earlier during a property inspection. I tried to glance at the dining room table, the last known location of Calvin's 9mm pistol. But it was dark inside and Calvin was blocking my view. I wasn't armed (as usual), and hadn't planned on interacting with anyone.

I stepped back into my truck, with my heart beating in my throat, rolled the window down and said, "What?"

He paused for a minute, "You called Tonya a liar."

"Calvin, Tonya said she was going to pay me and she didn't. That's lying."

Tonya barged outside, upset, "Mike you called me a liar and that really hurts! I'm not a liar, my phone got broken and I didn't have no way to call you to get you the money."

I looked at Calvin, his eyes darted away, "Calvin has my number, and he answered my call by mistake, then hung up on me when he realized who was calling him."

Calvin knitted his brow, "My phone was broke too."

"Let me guess, both of your phones are still broken, that's why I haven't heard from you.

I got a concerted "Yes." from them.

I started slowly driving away, "If your phones were broken, how did you know I said you were lying? You suck at lying, please stop doing it! I'll see you in court on Thursday."

They didn't show up to court and I won. The day the eviction was to be enforced I drove to the condo and looked around outside. There were fresh scratches on the front door and their patio furniture was gone. I called the number on the court order and talked to someone at the sheriff's office. "I am scheduled for an eviction this afternoon, but it looks like my tenants have gone. Do I have the right to enter my property?" The guy on the other end of the phone said, "Yes. But it's been kind of weird this month. We've had a bunch of people barricade themselves in and have had a lot of standoffs. A couple of them were bad."

I replied, "I'll wait."

An officer arrived later and I opened the door. The place was empty and in good shape. Tonya actually sent me a text a week or so after it was over and thanked me for being such a nice landlord. True story.

The following section outlines the Oklahoma City eviction process in a nutshell (I can only speak to the process in my town, yours may be quite different. Please do your own research):

You must properly notify your tenant with a five day notice to pay or quit. This notice can be sent as soon as the second day of the month if the tenants haven't paid rent by the first. The notice states that the tenant can either pay their rent, or move out in the next five (business) days or you will file an eviction. Certified mail (costs about $4.00 and has a green sticker) sent with the five day notice is considered proper notification. Don't bother paying extra for a signature or confirmation. You won't get either because people never pick it up. They know what's happening. I leave them a matter of fact message or tell them over the phone what I'm doing the day I send notice so they can start packing. Posting notice shows you are serious, and sometimes that's all it takes. If the tenants listed their parents as "emergency contacts" on the lease, I consider legal action to be an emergency. I call their mom and tell her too!

Once your five business days have gone by, you can head to the courthouse to schedule a hearing. In legal terms, an eviction is called a "Forcible Detainer and Entry." Your tenants must receive proper notification (again, a proof of service) which can be done either by certified mail, or served by the sheriff (for $50.00 more). In Oklahoma County you will get a court date for the next week.

I went through this process myself for that first eviction in order to learn. I explain the eviction process to new tenants before we sign a lease, both so they know how serious being late on rent is, and to help point out the gravity of signing a lease. I indicate to my new tenant that this lease is the document we will reference if a dispute arises between us. I tell them if they think anything is unfair, the time to discuss matters is prior to signing the lease.

Your tenant most likely won't show up to court. The day I went, there were roughly 100 evictions granted in less than an hour. Only about 15 tenants were present. Of that number, only a few of them got to speak before the judge cut them off and granted the owner their property back. In court, the judge called out the case number, asked if the landlord was present (and drops the case if they didn't show), then asked if the tenant was there. If a tenant was in the courtroom the judge asked, "Are you behind on your rent?" A reply of, "Yeah, but-" immediately was met by the judge raising her hand and saying, "Possession granted. Next case is..."

Once your Forcible Entry and Detainer is granted, the sheriff's office posts a 48 hour notice that they are going to come and get you.

I haven't had to go through with an eviction since my first. I usually offer a cash payment to tenants before I start paying money to the authorities. I feel I get my property back faster, cheaper and in better condition than I would through the legal system. I know I already said this at the beginning of the chapter. It's worth repeating. Paying people off makes moving a non-paying tenant a business decision, with no hard feelings. And, I shake the hand of an outgoing tenant after they take my payment. No matter what I'm thinking.

Chapter 14: Shake and Bake

After we closed on the $100,000.00 credit line (2014), my MLS search pinged a house on the same block as the "cursed" house. The new listing was for $25,000.00, and was a brick two bed, one bath 1000 square foot home across the street from a park. The comment section of the listing said, "...currently occupied, tenant pays $500 per month and wants to stay. Will show on Saturday mornings only." I drove by after work that day, sent a quick text to my realtor and had an appointment to see this property two days after it hit the market.

I showed up early and the tenant let me in. We looked around and I was stoked! It was a cute house, had a woman and her two older daughters living in it, and *I didn't have to fix anything*. The tenants wanted to stay, and the terms of their lease were harsher than the ones on mine (so I adopted some of them). I made a full price cash offer. I had the money, it was a good deal and I didn't want to screw anything up by trying to haggle over a relatively small amount of cash. This purchase, using 25% of my credit line money, was going to earn more than the minimum payment for the borrowed amount every month. Plus, the condo's mortgage was paid off and it was rented for $580.00 per month. And finally, I still had a good chunk of money left in my credit line. I inspected the house myself and didn't find any big problems so we closed as soon as the title company completed their work, about two weeks later.

At closing, the owners of the house arrived. The wife was the one signing the paperwork. While the seller and her realtor were in a conference room, the husband took me aside. He said, "We have another house that is much better than this one. It's rented section 8 for $750.00 per month. We want to sell, but don't want to list it. We will take $30,000.00 for it and you pay the closing costs." I wrote down his phone number.

After closing, I went straight to my new property. I brought a lease for the tenant to sign and slapped a business card magnet printed with my company name, phone number and PO Box on her refrigerator. I took all their phone numbers, and told them to start mailing payments to me, answered some questions, then left. It was awesome.

I exchanged phone calls with the couple that sold me the house. The husband was working on the wife to sell their other rented property. Landlording was her idea, but she was making her husband do all the handyman work (which he didn't want to do). Their business may have flourished if they had approached things differently, but I ended up with the fruits of their labor. We went ahead with the deal on their Section 8 house a couple of months later. I had been interested in working with Section 8, but didn't know very much about the program. So buying a house already on Section 8 was a great segue into the process.

I spent my $100,000.00 line of credit. I had several large expenses to take care of on various properties, but things were going well. My minimum monthly payment on the $100,000.00 credit line was $450.00. The amount of monthly rent I was receiving directly because of the credit line: $580.00 + $500.00 + $750.00 = $1,830.00. I could afford the occasional water heater and it was easy to pay our student loan bills (don't forget, we were getting rent from two other homes as well).

Also, the credit line was secured by the condo and the two other properties we had bought the year before. We owned the pair of houses I recently bought from that couple outright, which meant I had two more homes I could take to the bank!

Chapter 15: A Copy of a Copy

The next year (2015) I headed back to my banker again. We re-structured the debt scheme into a $100,000.00 note amortized over 15 years with a balloon payment at five years*. We then took out another credit line against the two houses we bought in 2014. The new credit line was for $42,000.00 (I'd bought those two houses for $25,000.00 and $30,000.00 = $55,000.00) - each time we financed out a property it was only for a percentage of the appraised value, not the full amount. Like the degradation experienced by making copies of copies, our buying power was losing resolution.

*A balloon payment is a large payment that is due at a certain point of a loan. At our interest rate, we will have paid around $25,000.00 of the principle after five years of payments, leaving a balance of $75,000.00 due at that time. This will force us into starting a new 15 year note at (most likely) a higher interest rate.

The bank was not about to stick its neck out too far. Lenders always keep in mind they may have to take your properties back and sell them. So this marked the last year of being able to expand our holdings using credit lines alone. Even though we were buying houses at good prices, only being able to cash out a fraction of that purchase price each time left us with less money every cycle. Appraisers can see how much you spent on the house you bought, so when they do an appraisal on your property, the number they arrive at is usually close to what you recently paid. We were fine with that since our little company had met all of its founding objectives. Our rentals were comfortably covering all their expenses AND our student loan payments. I simply wanted to buy *one more house*.

When I'm not in buying mode, I still watch my MLS feed, just not as obsessively. I see houses pop up, then come off in a week or so. Others have been out there for months. I keep tabs on what a "good deal" is for me, and I don't let one getting away bother me. The ones I want only come up every month or so, but I take solace in the fact that they keep on coming. "The deal of the century comes up once a week!" is a mantra I often hear at our real estate meetings. I repeat that quote when a house fitting my parameters comes along and I'm not ready to buy. I have gained perspective, which helps me stay calm.

And, so far, every time I've been ready to buy a house something worthwhile appears. 2015 proved to be no different. As soon as my money was available, a four bed, two bath, brick house popped up for $30,000.00. It was "currently occupied" and the tenant paid $650.00 per month, but was moving out. The landlord had passed away and the family wanted to split the estate. We offered $28,000.00 (and for them to get rid of their tenants) and they took it! I hadn't seen a house this good for this cheap all year and I was excited.

Section 8 became increasingly tempting. We were getting tired of some of our regular (not Section 8) tenants having excuses instead of rent at the first of the month. It was stressful threatening people with homelessness every month. Stepping back, we analyzed who our tenants were. Who wanted to live in the low income part of town? The answer was simple; low income people. We could continue to rent to those who were barely scraping by, or commit to those on government assistance. My Section 8 house had been a nice source of steady income with little headache, so we decided to venture into Section 8 with the new place. Plus, I loved the idea of paying back government debt with money I received from a government program. It was poetic.

Chapter 16: Section 8 is Great!*

If you don't mind the hassle up front.

I'd heard rumors of what a pain Section 8 was to deal with, but my experience with my existing Section 8 house was quite the contrary.

Most of my tenants are very appreciative of Section 8 and me. Everyone wins with Section 8; the tenant gets a free (or rent reduced) house, and the landlord gets their rent direct deposited the first of each month.

However, getting started with Section 8 can be a hassle.

During an annual inspection on my Section 8 house, an inspector found a few issues which he deemed were "tenant responsibilities" to repair. I decided to abate the problems myself for two reasons: First, I didn't want an interruption to my income over some silly minor repairs. The second reason was to learn the layout of my house. I'd only been inside this property for ten minutes up to that point. My Section 8 tenant had four "two legged pets". Children can be more destructive than a Rottweiler! One door was kicked in, another was missing knobs, a cabinet door was broken, and a bunch of sealant had been torn away from the glass block windows in the bathroom. Also, the smoke detector was making the intermittent "chirp" signaling a dying battery. The house was pretty dark because many of the lights were burnt out. I spent about 4 hours and $100.00 fixing these issues. I should have charged the tenant for the repairs, but decided to do it for free as a token of good will. Hell, I made $750.00 a month off the place and had yet to do anything more than occasionally drive by the property to verify it hadn't burned down.

In my experience, low income tenants often do not replace burnt out light bulbs or dying smoke detector batteries. Both of which are big issues for Section 8 inspectors. Now that LEDs have come down in price, I'm using them so I don't have to deal with burned out bulbs later. I also buy 10 year smoke detectors for the same reason. I choose my battles.

My area's Section 8 website is quite obtuse when it comes to providing adequate landlord information on what constitutes a house that passes inspection. A few other landlords gave me some advice, and I found what I could, but I still failed my first few inspections. Here's what I can tell you:

Section 8 is a program set up by the federal government which allows each state to assist very low income families with housing. The state has a Public Housing Agency funded by the US Department of Housing and Urban Development (HUD). Tenants can choose to live in housing projects or find private residences with landlords willing to participate in the program. A great many tenants would prefer to avoid "the projects", so landlords usually have a decent pool of qualified individuals to work with. My (limited)

experience has found the ranks of Section 8 l
filled with single mothers trying to raise thei
Search online for "housing choice voucher p
learn more about Section 8.

It is not discrimination to say, "No Section 8
allowed" on your advertisements or when you speak to
people. According to the Fair Housing Act, you cannot
discriminate against: Race or Color, National Origin,
Religion, Sex, Familial Status (whether someone has
children or not) or Persons with Disabilities. You can
weed out slobs, people who have been evicted in the
past, smokers, people with pet rattlesnakes, people who
don't have enough money or those that suffer from
halitosis if you want. As long as you are not targeting a
protected group, you are not "discriminating" according
to the law.

If you decide to accept Section 8 tenants, prepare
to work with a Section 8 inspector. Frustratingly,
inspectors are everyday people who have their own
individual biases and hot button topics. If you fail an
inspection with one inspector, they may not be assigned
to your house for the re-inspection. All inspectors must
go through the same training and are supposed to be
looking for the same items. Safety is their main
priority, and it can be taken to an extreme, depending
on your inspector. Items your inspector is looking for
come from guidelines set by the federal government
(HUD) and are subject to change. These items include:

Every window in the house originally designed to
open must be able to open, stay open without a prop or

er device, easily close, and lock with its own lock. Your window can't rely on aftermarket thumb screw locks, broomsticks, or makeshift locks. Windows must be free of cracks, peeling paint and broken seals. Windows must be sealed from the elements. Torn screens are to be removed or replaced. Windows with a window air conditioning unit do not have to open, but there should be another form of egress from the room in case of fire. Burglar bars must be easy to open from the inside without a special tool, or removed for fire safety.

Roofs must be free of leaks.

The yard must be mowed, and even if your lease says the tenant has to do it, you still better make sure it's mowed prior to inspection.

Exterior doors must be weather sealed (shut the door, turn off the lights, if any daylight is visible around the door - you fail). You can use cheap sticky foam strips from the hardware store to accomplish this - keep some handy in case a piece falls off during your inspection!

Houses built before 1978 may have been painted with lead based paint. Therefore, if your house was built before 1978, no peeling paint is allowed anywhere and no paint chips can be on the ground outside.

You must have handrails at steps, even if they don't lead anywhere. There is a set of five concrete steps behind one of my houses that leads to a now walled off back door. We had to install a handrail or get rid of the steps.

Anything broken has to be removed, repaired, or replaced (even if it's out of reach). I had a house fail over a broken piece of guttering ten feet off the ground.

The electrical system of your house should have properly grounded electrical outlets, if available. If you have an old house that hasn't been re-wired with grounded outlets, but someone has replaced the old two prong outlets with three prong outlets, you either need to go through the hassle of running copper wire from every outlet to a grounding rod, or to the copper pipes in your house, or you can change the outlets back to two prongs (which are still sold at the hardware store or online). Outlets cannot be broken at all. There can't be any tiny cracks in the cover plate, no broken spot at the bottom by the grounding hole where the plug got yanked out. The same goes for light switches and cable TV plates. There also cannot be a gap between the outlet cover and the wall - hardware stores sell quite large outlet and switch covers for this purpose. Every light must work, including outdoor lights. If the light fixture to the back yard floodlights is all corroded and doesn't work anymore you can replace it or remove it. Power lines cannot be in anyone's reach. If there are lines hanging low in your back yard, call the utility company. They usually fix problems like that for free, or they will tell you to call an electrician. Your breaker box can't have any gaps in it between the front panel and the breakers inside.

Your plumbing should work and not leak. You need hot and cold running water to the kitchen and bathrooms. Section 8 does not allow dripping faucets or chronically running toilets. Toilets must be secured to the floor, and suffer no broken seat covers or cracked seats. The wall under your cabinet should not have any holes in it; all gaps around pipes must be sealed.

A Section 8 water heater cannot have leaks, it must have a drain pan underneath it with the proper diameter drain tube. Gas water heaters cannot be in a fully enclosed cabinet, and must be on a stand if in a bedroom. According to HUD, the water heater must have tubing for potable (drinking) water connected to the Temperature Pressure Relief (TPR) valve no more than 6" above the floor. I know, right? Every time I want a nice cup of water for my hot cocoa powder, I throw open the water heater cabinet, stick my mug under the TPR valve and trip the lever to dump water straight out of the tank. Don't you? Worse yet, there are several types of pipe to choose from. A big problem can occur if you have a pipe that is painted black. Certain types of black metal pipe are made for potable water, and if the inspector can't tell what kind it is (they don't waste much effort looking) they will fail your house. This happened to me. My water heater passed the initial inspection, but the house failed on a couple of other miniscule issues. A follow up inspection occurred and a different inspector opened up the water heater cabinet, saw a black metal pipe and failed the house! My plumber called the Section 8 office after I told him he just cost me $850.00, and the

Section 8 office said there was nothing they could do about it. The supervisor agreed with the plumber that the heater was to code, but said the inspectors have the final say on whether or not your house passes. The inspector made the decision in a matter of seconds and had the rest of the hour off. The lesson here is: PUT A NON THREADED COPPER PIPE ON YOUR TPR DRAIN! Everyone knows what copper is. Copper will pass every time.

According to HUD, your bathroom can't have mold or rust issues. If there is a rust spot on your bath sink, your house will fail. A quick shot of spray enamel will magically cover rust. Fiberglass Reinforced Plastic (FRP) board is a quick, permanent way to cover failing wallpaper, peeling paint, or whatever else is causing an eyesore around your shower. Loose bathroom tiles are also verboten, so glue them back in place. If your bathroom features an old gas heater, get rid of it, cap the line (if it's still connected) and remove the thing. Then cover the hole with some thin plywood, FRP, or the like. If there are multiple bathrooms in your house only one must have the full array of bathroom amenities which include a sink, toilet, and a place to bathe.

Every burner on your kitchen stove must work. If it's a gas stove, every burner must light using the cooktop's ignition system (no matches). The oven must work. Any defunct built in appliances must be removed. I had an old cabinet mounted double oven in a place, put in a new free standing electric range and the house failed because of the double oven. If your place has a broken garbage disposal, trash it or replace it. The refrigerator should be clean and working. Electric outlets near the sink need to be Ground Fault Circuit Interrupter (GFCI) outlets. If you are wondering whether or not your regular outlet is too close to a sink, just upgrade it to GFCI, $10.00 is a cheap exchange for a month's rent. A fridge, sink, stove and a working light are all that are required in a kitchen.

Personally, I feel the less, the better when it comes to appliances. Do you want to be in the free appliance repair business, or make money as a landlord? When a couple looks at one of my homes and one person asks me, "What about a dish washer?" I always gesture toward the other person and say, "There he is!" I recommend a portable dishwasher for those houses that don't have one, saying, "Then you can take it with you when you move 10 years from now." I don't buy refrigerators with ice makers either. It's another potential water leak disaster and I don't want to fix ice makers.

I'm changing my strategy regarding amenities in my Section 8 homes. Now when someone moves out, I eliminate as many potential problems as possible. Ceiling fans get removed and replaced with simple, cheap light fixtures. Fans are not required by Section 8, but if one has a broken blade or other problem the landlord has to fix it. Plus, your tenant is not going to wait until their next inspection to complain. It will be your problem the instant a fan goes off kilter. If my tenant requires a fan in their bedroom, they can buy one at the store for a few dollars and set it on their dresser.

I've also decided to do away with laundry hookups. Washing machines can dump over 20 gallons of water into your sewer line very quickly. If you have an old, partially clogged waste line, a washer may be able to dump more water than the pipes can handle. Waste water will fill your bathtub or shower and cause the toilet to overflow. My plumber charges $120.00 every time he has to snake a sewer line, and this usually occurs at houses which have a washing machine running at the time of the complaint. Also, I do not want to gamble on someone else's appliances and supply lines to remain leak free. My Section 8 tenants can go to the laundromat, and my plumber can sleep in on the weekends.

Roaches, fleas, or mice will fail your house. My lease states the tenant is responsible for pest control. I don't want to get a phone call every time someone sees a spider. But I will cover bug spraying for the sake of passing inspection, and to provide a sanitary home for new tenants to move into.

Smoke alarms need to be near bedrooms. If you have a hall that leads to three bedroom doors (in a three bed house), one alarm in that hall will work. If you have a separate mother-in-law setup, then you will need a smoke alarm outside that door, too.

Fire extinguishers are not required, but I have one in every kitchen. The property your tenant saves might be your own!

Each Section 8 office maintains a voluntary list of landlords' phone numbers. I have found one office in particular that I prefer to work with, so I keep my number on their list. I receive a call or two every day from someone looking to rent a house. My voicemail asks that they text me their name, voucher size, and phone number. Then my recorded message says I will call them back when a unit becomes available. Even if I don't anticipate a vacancy, things happen, and I always have a list of fresh phone numbers to call in the event of a surprise vacancy.

So far, Section 8 has been good to me. I have been able to provide affordable housing to an underserved population, and most of my tenants really appreciate working with me. I receive a steady stream of rent in a part of town where this can be a rare occurrence from someone not on government assistance. Section 8 IS great!

Chapter 17: Narrowing it All Down

Hopefully I haven't scared anyone off the idea of real estate investing. If I did, I hope it was for the right reasons. Maybe I saved someone who thought this would be a cake walk a few thousand bucks. I wrote this book to inspire and help people avoid pitfalls I had to overcome. My enthusiasm got the best of me more than once, but I'm still here – probably because of it. Indecision is a business killer. If you want to get into real estate, pick a type of investment and stick with it until you are good at that particular style. I sucked at first, I bought the wrong house to start out with, and I took a beating. If I had completely changed course following my initial mistake, I would have screwed up something new, and disaster would have been right around the corner. I would have been worse off than when I started, owing more money than ever with nothing to fall back on.

In this game the field is vast. There is so much to choose from in the world of real estate investing, and real estate books often give information on tons of different investing techniques. Reading a bunch of advice books turned me schizophrenic. Should I do a lease purchase deal, a short sale, a contract assignment, go to a tax sale, flip a house, get a foreclosure list, find something online, use a realtor, put signs on street corners and my car, mail out postcards, or get a megaphone and start shouting from the window of my truck?

What kind of property do I want to buy? A house, a multiplex, an apartment complex, commercial property, an empty lot, a trailer park, a marina, a bridge, or a rocket launch pad? Because I'm going to the moon! What part of town am I going to work? High class, low class, no class, everywhere or concentrate on a certain area?

Ok. Breathe...

Take it easy. Narrow everything down to your objective. My objective was to use rentals to pay back my student loans. I didn't have a crew, I didn't want a partner, I was in it for the long term and my budget was whatever I could scrape together.

Here's a synopsis of some investment options:

House Flipping

Woo hoo! Flipping houses is really fun to watch on TV, fortunes are made and they make it look so easy. In real life, you have to be very connected, very knowledgeable, and very ready to take a loss. I remember when those shows first aired, the disclaimer on one of them - the last sentence was, "...if you do this, you will lose money." That line has been softened to, "...flipping houses is risky." Flippers don't lose money every time, but it happens often. Flipping involves speculation, luck, and a very extensive knowledge of the market. You need a good crew of (cheap) workers and everything must go just right, or you will turn a small fortune into a smaller one. Unless you are a contractor and know your market very well, you would do well to avoid this method of investing. One big thing they don't mention on the flipping shows is taxes. If you pull off a flip, after all those weeks (more likely months) of stress, you will give about half your proceeds back to Uncle Sam in the form of short term capital gains tax. Flipping is WORK. Something I try to avoid if I can help it. Once you finish your flip, you have to use the money on your next project to keep going. Find another house, analyze the neighborhood, get the crew out, make 1000 choices, and spend more than you estimated.

I've met several flippers at the REIA meetings. They are major risk takers, appear nervous, and get consolation from other flippers in the group by exchanging stories of woe. Yes, they make money, but flipping is a full time job. I'm not saying I would never flip a house, but the income is too sporadic to make regular monthly payments, and the tax scenario doesn't work to my advantage.

Land Speculation

To speculate on land, buy an empty lot and hope someday it becomes a subdivision, or whatever. For example, you can buy a broke down old farm, go to the city planner's office and try to get it zoned commercial or residential (for a fee, of course). When the payday arrives, it could be sweet! Until then, you have a patch of mud and weeds. Speculation provides no regular income. And you may be long dead before anyone wants to buy the place. In the meantime, you still have to pay taxes on your lot (and keep it mowed if it's in town).

Commercial Properties

Commercial properties are impressive. They are big and expensive, can have very long term tenants and range from small strip centers to office parks and up to shopping malls and big multistory buildings. Unlike houses, these properties are worth whatever they are bringing in for rent.

The owner of a commercial property needs to be very business savvy as many small businesses fail and, obviously, the landlord can't collect rent if their tenant is bankrupt. You need to evaluate your potential tenant's business and see if it is a good fit for your property, or if their business idea is a reasonable one to start out with. You want your commercial property to be filled to 100% capacity as often as possible, but realize these places can stay empty for YEARS. If you buy one that is full and then tenant Moses shows up the day after you close and takes all his people (your tenants) with him, you would have a huge bill to pay on a place that is worth NOTHING.

Commercial buildings have big air conditioning units on the roof right next to each other for the convenience of copper thieves. If the bandits come milling about on your roof in the middle of the night (because no one is at their commercial property at 3am) you will be out tens of thousands of dollars while they recycle $100 worth of copper.

Look around while driving. You will see tons of commercial places empty and for rent. They are maintenance headaches. You still have to mow, you still have to clean the windows, keep utilities on, pay taxes and insurance, pick up trash and keep weeds from growing in your empty parking lot.

If your commercial property is rented, you get to deal with issues between tenants. For example, the Christian bookstore owner might have a problem with you leasing to a lingerie shop two doors down. There are also parking issues, business turf wars, tenants talking to each other and one of them finding out the other guy is paying $4.00 less per square foot, forklifts poking holes through walls, chemical smells from a paint shop bothering the telemarketers next door, shared bathrooms (who's going to clean them?), brokers wanting a fat commission to lease one of your spaces to their client, someone "tripping" on the sidewalk in front of your anchor store and filing a big lawsuit against you and your tenant. If the city decides they need to widen the street in front of your complex, and redo the utilities underneath while they have the road demolished, it will be almost impossible for your tenant's customers to reach them. The customers will take their business elsewhere and kill your little strip mall. You can't rent to businesses that aren't making money. You also have to worry about a big company constructing a hot new building taking the cream of the crop tenants away and making your place worthless.

I know some commercial guys. This stuff happens.

There are certainly a lot of people who have gotten rich from commercial property. I'm sure they would be quick to tell you that getting to that point was a hassle. Is making any kind of money a hassle? Of course it is. Choose your problems wisely. I want my stress level to be as low as possible, the headaches small and the risks manageable.

Multiunit Homes

How about multiplexes? Duplexes, triplexes, quadriplexes, etcetera-plexes. Tons of rent on one property, right? You could buy a duplex, live in one side and rent the other half out to cover your mortgage payment.

Yes, but...

Tenants call these places "my apartment ". People move out of apartments. People smoke outside their apartments, and have fights in the night bothering their neighbors (your other tenants). Who is an annoyed tenant going to talk to? The obnoxious drunk neighbor, or the landlord? *You* get that call after the bars close. As with commercial properties, you have the problem of tenants talking to each other. What if you had to drop the rent a little to follow Section 8 guidelines, or just to be nice to someone who needs a little break? The others will want the same deal. What if you have a party animal? A drug dealer? A bass player? With a single family home, at least the problem is isolated. There is no opportunity for a move out plague to spread through your houses. You also have to do common area maintenance on multiplexes. Mowing, litter removal, snow removal, and parking fights are but a few of the additional responsibilities the landlord has to deal with.

On the upside multiplexes put all your tenants in one location. If something is broken you know right where you are headed. Also, a 20 unit apartment complex only has one roof and far fewer windows than 20 houses. I'm considering buying one now that I have processes in place and connections I can call on, but I recommend single family homes to new real estate investors. Get good at dealing with one or two tenants and properties before you buy an apartment complex. If you decide being a landlord isn't your cup of tea, it's far easier to unload a house or two than a multiunit dwelling.

Condominiums/Town Homes

No mowing! No exterior maintenance! But you get to pay Home Owner's Association fees that cost several times more than a yard guy would charge (which your tenant should be paying for anyway). Speaking of the HOA, they might not be too happy for you to rent out your unit. Insurance companies want to charge more to insure properties that are less than 60% owner occupied. Your tenant may not respect the covenants of the HOA, and you are the liable owner. Tenants call condos "the apartment". Do I have one? Yes. Do I wish it was a house? Yes!!! I spend $100 per month on HOA fees at a place that does almost nothing. They are supposed to maintain the fences (they don't). Do you think my tenant cares who is supposed to fix the fence? My tenant wanted the fence fixed as it was broken and rotten, so I shelled out several hundred bucks. $100 every month of my rental income is thrown away to the HOA which eats into my profits. It's terrible. I still make money off the place but I hate the HOA fees. In my town you can't get $100 more per month in rent for a $25,000.00 condo than you can for a house of the same price. Quite the contrary, I can get more out of an affordable house than my condominium. Condos can really cut into your cash flow*. I've owned this condo for 18 years. That's $100 per month or $1,200 per year x 18 years = $21,600.00 spent on HOA fees!!! For that I've had a meager strip of grass mowed, 3 hedges occasionally cut and the place painted twice. The parking lot is full of potholes and the complex has really gone downhill, but the dues remain and are likely going to increase to keep the place afloat. I am not a fan of condominiums. I know people who are, and they are nice people even though they are wrong.

*Cash flow is the money you have left after expenses. If you have a house that rents for $1,000.00 per month, and your payments, average repairs, and insurance add up to $900.00, then you have $100.00 per month of positive cash flow. Cash flow can also be negative, which sucks. Avoid negative cash flow.

Trailer Houses/Manufactured Homes

I don't know trailers. I read a great book about them called "Mobile Home Wealth" by Salman Velvel[5]. It was a very interesting, entertaining read and I drew some landlording advice from it. But I have never lived in a trailer, owned one, or had much to do with trailers. My impression is they are poorly built and the resale value of mobile homes is abysmal. I looked into investing in trailers, but they currently aren't my cup of tea.

Single Family Homes

There are tons of these. Most everyone wants to live in a house. Tenants call houses "home". They plant flowers in front and stick little solar powered lights around the porch. They usually stay for years. Who can an investor buy a single family home from? Anybody! If you are buying an apartment complex, multiplex or commercial property, you are dealing with another investor, same thing when you sell. Who can you sell a house to if you need some money? Anybody!

People are sometimes motivated to get rid of a house. I've bought a couple of them because some relative died, the family is out of state and the heirs are liquidating assets to split the proceeds.

Tenants in a house have privacy and are willing to accept some responsibilities, like mowing the yard and picking up trash outside. Houses are cute, they have curb appeal and the rules to buy and sell single family homes are standardized. Also, you can buy whatever you need to fix a house at most any hardware store. Finally, houses often appreciate in value.

I wanted good old single family homes. I still do. It's my thing.

Now, where to buy one?

Oklahoma City is a big town. To narrow my search I looked at rental websites, then at home buying sites to see how much houses cost compared to their rental take. I needed some good cash flow to make my plan work. That meant cheap houses, so to speak.

Why do I buy cheap houses? Let's say I have $100,000.00 to invest. I can take that to a middle class part of (this) town and buy one 3 bedroom, 1.5 bath house with a 1 car garage and rent it for around $1,100.00 a month ($13,200.00 per year). Not too shabby.

Or, I can go to the poorer part of town, buy three houses, have cash left over and pull down a lot more in rent. The last house I purchased cost me $28,000.00. It is a four bed, two bath, brick home rented to a Section 8 tenant for $850.00 per month (That's $10,200.00 per year). If I had three of those, my monthly income would be $2,550.00 ($30,600.00 per year = *2.3 times more rental income than the suburbs*) from the same $100,000.00 amount invested. In the cash flow game, the lower income area smokes the suburbs every time. If they were 100% rented and no repairs were needed, my houses would buy themselves every three years. These figures fit my business plan. Not only will I cover my monthly student loan bill, I can get out of real estate debt quickly. You are going to have to ride out a 30 year mortgage on that house in the suburbs, and not have enough to pay your real estate debt and your student loan debt at the same time.

The trade off with affordable houses? Appreciation, and wear and tear. Cheap houses don't gain value like suburban homes. Expect to regularly repair your homes in the poorer part of town, but by using cheaper fixtures the repairs aren't usually very costly.

In summary, I can't emphasize the standard single family home enough. They are plentiful, desirable, easy to buy and easy to sell. By starting out with single family homes, a neophyte landlord will be more likely to succeed and suffer fewer complications in this business.

Chapter 18: Getting Money

If you don't have access to your own startup money (home equity, 401k loan, cash stuffed in your mattress), then you have to find it. There are trillions of dollars out there and you only need a few thousand to get started. Study your market. Know you are going to succeed and draft a business plan. If you have awesome credit and a great income, then a bank may be where you start. Even if the bank says no, that's just one "no" closer to the bank that says yes. Are you worried about using your home equity to become a landlord? Good! It's scary to put yourself on the line. That's why there are relatively few landlords out there.

I started my real estate venture by raising money from family. No, I'm not some rich kid. My mother didn't go to college and she didn't hit the lottery or invest in the stock market at just the right time. She had access to money she had dutifully saved, and equity in her home she wasn't using. Also, she knew I would follow through with the plan I constructed. The idea I pitched didn't require some improbable effort to pay her loans back. I presented an elegant solution to a problem and my mother helped me out. Once she invested in my company, my cousin became intrigued and contributed as well. Being a parent, I can totally understand why my mother would put so much at stake for me. I would do the same for my kids if I felt they were motivated enough to carry a plan through (This is easy for me to say right now, my kids aren't big enough to ask for thousands of dollars yet.).

So what if your folks don't have a dime to their name and neither do you?   How can you start a real estate venture in that scenario? Make your business plan. Know you are going to succeed, and have a folder full of information ready to show anyone who is willing to listen to you. Tell everyone about your plan. You will be surprised where money can come from. Friends, coworkers, and acquaintances may surprise you. You will never know if you don't ask. Remember, this is a business thing, don't take someone telling you no personally. In some states, you can get cash loans from personal lending websites, and if you have a real estate deal that is good enough, you can convince someone from across the country or the world to finance you. Read lots of real estate investing books, they are packed with ideas. All you have to do is put your first deal together. The next deal will come later, and will be easier to pull off. Eat the elephant one bite at a time. If you don't make a lot of money at your job, you may only have to own one or two rental homes to make your income based student loan payments anyway.

I have a collection of fortune cookie papers taped to my refrigerator and I look at them often. I like simplifying, and sometimes reducing everything down to a sentence on a strip of paper is the best way to pass along a great idea. My favorites include:

"I would rather try to do something great and fail, than attempt to do nothing and succeed."

"Obstacle - The thing you see when you are not looking at your GOAL."

"You will have gold pieces by the bushel."

Take the risk that most people don't. Having fear is natural, and conquering your fears is deeply satisfying. Everyone doubts themselves sometimes, just shake it off and keep your eyes on the prize.

As a new anesthesia provider, I thought it was strange how different types of people responded to the stress of going into surgery. I've taken care of people from all walks of life and it seemed to me as though those with the least to lose were the most concerned about the "...you could die." part of our pre-operative talk. On the other hand, millionaire entrepreneurs laugh and chat with friends and family prior to being wheeled back to the operating room, even if the surgery they are about to have is quite serious. The people who never took a serious risk in their life, who didn't even move out of their parent's house at adulthood, normally make a tremendous deal out of a small surgery. This puzzled me until I started buying houses. Business is all about managing risk. Entrepreneurs make risk calculations all the time. Surgery is also a calculated risk, if the benefit outweighs the consequences of not operating, the entrepreneur makes the call, knows it's the best decision given the information on hand, and moves on. I don't doubt the entrepreneur is concerned about their life. They've made their decision and would rather crack a few jokes or have a meaningful conversation while they can. Come what may.

Be the person that takes the chance. Your future self will thank you. Yes, it will take several years for your properties to buy themselves, but think about the position you would be in *right now* if you had bought a rental house five years ago and now owned it outright. Think about what was happening to you five years in the past and what a short time ago that felt like. Time happens no matter what you do. You didn't wait until you could save up for that college degree. Why wait and save money for a house that can make its own payments? The sooner you take advantage of time, the better off you will be in the future.

Chapter 19: Tips to Keep You Sane

Don't let your rentals run your life! If you spend every free moment toiling away at your houses and running all over town, you will **hate** being a landlord. Build systems for everything you do. Reevaluate what you are doing frequently. The income from rental houses is supposed to be *passive income* and I strive to keep it that way.

I downloaded a free time keeper app for my phone and clocked in every time I did anything regarding my real estate. I found I was putting in several hours a month driving to and from the post office, neurotically checking the PO Box for rent checks. All it did was waste gas and increase my blood pressure when I found (after checking every day starting at the 28th) that someone hadn't gotten their rent in by the 5th. I could shave hours off my total real estate time investment every month by reducing those trips

Everyone knows when rent is due. I tell my tenants the postmark date on their envelope counts as the day they paid. If the post office is a little slow but you put it in the mail on time, then no late fee. So why sweat it when someone is late? Sure, if I'm about to pull the eviction trigger on someone then I'll pop by the post office more often, but regular month to month stuff can wait. I only want to check my mail once a month. I head to the PO Box around the 15th. All the stragglers have gotten their rent in and I get a fistful of checks. My blood pressure stays low, and my gas tank stays full. I take all the checks, lay them on top of the envelopes they came in (so you can see the postmark date and their return address) and take a picture with my phone. It's hard to argue the rent got lost in the mail when the check was cut on the sixth and the postmark is from the eighth. Furthermore, I've never had a rent check actually get lost in the mail. I tell the tenant the late fee will be waived if they get a correctly addressed envelope back that is postmarked before the due date. It's never happened.

When the check doesn't show and the B.S. gets deep, I tell them to meet me with rent in hand at a place and time of my convenience or I'm starting the eviction process. Don't go to someone's (Your!) house, to pick up late rent. You think your blood pressure gets high when you go to the PO Box and its empty? Just wait until you go to an obviously occupied house to collect and no one responds to your knocking. Don't be that sucker.

Make sure you buy cash flowing houses. If being a landlord costs you money you will hate it, even if a rental only costs you a few dollars every month. First of all, you can't pay your loans back, and secondly waiting 30 years (until a mortgage is paid off) to turn a profit is a no-win situation. I invest in the poorer part of town because of the huge return on these types of properties.

Put forth a professional appearance. I don't dress up in a three piece suit, but I have business cards and mail a very official looking statement to my tenants every month. You can make nice looking business cards with a desktop computer using pop out business card paper. Something about those little pieces of paper gives you instant credibility.

I mail rent statements on the 20th of the month. They are a friendly reminder that the first of the month is coming. I include the statement (modeled after my cable bill) and a payment envelope pre-printed with my PO Box address (tenants buy their own stamps). I played around with the arrangement of the address placement so the address shows through the windows on a double window envelope. Here's my configuration:

Company logo in center with mailing address and phone number

Date 11/20/####

Tenant's address

Monthly rent $### (or "Tenant Portion" if Section 8).

Previous Balance: $###

Rent Received: $### (postmarked xx/xx, thank you!)

Late Fee: $##

November Rent Due. $###

Total Due: $###

(The bottom fits in envelope windows on left)

Company Name

PO Box ###

Xxx, xx. #####

                        Total due 12/1/####: $###

Tenant, Tenant

123 Address St

City City, ST, ######

The statements are saved in my word processing program. I copy the previous month's statements over and edit them to the current month, mainly just switching a couple of dates. There is probably a faster way of generating statements, but this method has served me well.

In an ideal month, I go to the PO Box on the 15th, bring the envelopes home, snap pictures, and put a deposit together. I use a self-customizable rubber stamp with "For deposit only to XXX LLC, account ######", to speed up the process. Then I record the deposit on my bookkeeping software, and generate rent statements to go out on the 20th. The entire procedure takes about two hours, including driving.

I keep a couple of lock boxes in my vehicle. The kind I like have two combinations, one to access the key door, the other for the hasp that goes around the door knob (these boxes never go missing). They come in handy more often than you would think. I almost never have to waste my time meeting anyone at my properties. I've paid my plumber thousands of dollars to do more jobs than I care to recall and I have no idea what he looks like! If a tenant calls with a problem, I check it out, then put a lockbox on the door if there is a chance they won't be home for the repair. Legally, you must always have permission to enter, or at least post proper notice, but never has a tenant given me grief about someone coming out to fix something they complained about. Also, an empty property always gets a lockbox. Handymen, trade professionals, exterminators, and inspectors can all gain access to work inside my rentals while I'm elsewhere.

The lockbox is fantastic when a house needs carpet.

Here's how most people go about the process: They drive to the carpet store, start looking around, wait for a salesman to come over, then listen to a sales pitch on some expensive carpet they didn't really want. Once they've settled on flooring, the salesman gets out the schedule and books an estimate. Three days later, the estimator arrives at the house, spends a half hour measuring, talks for a while, then leaves. The carpet store calls the next day with the final cost and requires payment before the order is placed. They book an installation which requires another trip to the house. The homeowner meets the installer at the house once stock has arrived. It takes half a day to lay the carpet and viola, new flooring.

Now, here's how I go about the carpet buying process: I call the carpet store saying, "I need some landlord grade carpet at one of my rent houses. Gimme the cheapest stuff you got, I don't care what color it is as long as it's brown-ish. The address is.....the lockbox combination is 1234, my debit card number is....." And I'm done. It takes less than five minutes.

The first time you use a lockbox, you will know it already paid for itself.

I hold "open house" sessions when I have a place ready to rent. I quickly tired of people setting up viewings which they then didn't show up for, or came late, or wasted an hour of my life when they had no intention of renting the place. Open houses are great. If someone really wants your place they will change their schedule to see it. Usually several people rush our houses when we open the door. It's a great feeling! When I place an ad for a property, the last line of the write up says, "We will be holding an open house on Saturday, Month, Day, from 1-2pm. Please bring a

114

valid photo ID and $20 cash for the application fee so we may do a background check." I can easily change the last line in the ad if I don't get a qualified applicant the first week. The background check is solid gold. People who have been evicted, or who know they aren't otherwise going to pass a background check, certainly aren't going to waste their own money on one. Charge whatever you want, some people use professional agencies to check their tenant's backgrounds. $20.00 seems to work well for us. Any odd numbers and you have to make change. I have found simple internet searches are adequate, so I don't hire it out. Your local on demand court records database is a free way to check backgrounds and provides lots of information. Facebook is another good source as so many people leave their profiles public. It's fun to play the investigator.

I use the Kwikset Smart Key® lock set on all entry doors of my houses. The ability to re-key any lock at any time is awesome. With this system, you can change your locks in five minutes for free. I buy the brass version, because presently they are the most affordable option. It costs about $40.00 for each door, so the initial investment is high compared to locks that require replacement every time you change tenants. By your second tenant these locksets will have paid for themselves. I had a coworker tell me that his locksmith said the Smart Key® locks are easy to pick. Maybe they are easy to pick, or maybe locksmiths don't like doorknobs that can be rekeyed without their assistance. No matter how good your lock is, it won't stop someone from throwing a rock through a window. Unless you have a steel door and frame most anyone can kick in a door. Breaking and entering usually entails breaking something! I doubt very many burglars waste their time picking locks anyway.

To reduce break-ins, don't buy the cheap house that sits right next to an apartment complex. That house is cheap because it gets broken into *all the time*. Several old school landlords have told me to avoid a purchase like that and I have heeded their sage advice.

I get four keys for each house. Two go to the tenant. One stays labeled on my keychain in my vehicle. The fourth is kept on a key tag at my house. If a tenant loses their keys, I make two copies of a key and charge them $10.00. If something comes up at a house, I pull my key off my keychain and put it in the lockbox. No need to trek across town. It should go without saying, but don't give a tenant who loses keys the last key and then expect them to make a copy. Keep your two keys at all times. I have a few sets of extra keys ready to go. With the smart key system you can rotate keys through your properties if needed. After all, you are the only person who knows what key goes where. I could have all my houses keyed identically, no one would be the wiser, and I don't advertise to my tenants where my other properties are.

The smartphone is the landlord's office; I do almost everything on my phone. I use it for the bulk of my word processing, usually emailing the results to myself for posterity, and to do a final polish on my PC before printing. Occasionally, I will print straight from my phone. I send emails and text messages regarding my rentals from my phone throughout the day. I maintain a spreadsheet of my check register on my phone. Using the camera, I take pictures of prospective tenants ID's and documentation. I'll take pictures of leases and photos of my properties right after they've been made ready so I can post a "for rent" advertisement. I take pictures of problems and text them to my handyman, plumber, or electrician, saving me a thousand spoken words each time. If an item needs to be a certain size, I'll lay a tape measure beside it so no one has to guess what I'm trying to say. I always take ID pictures of prospective tenants when I hold an open house in an occupied unit to dissuade anyone who may be casing the place.

Get a Google Voice account. It's a great way to separate your landlording from all other aspects of your life. Google voice is an Internet phone connection which runs on a computer and works with a smartphone app. Google Voice gives you a second voicemail for your same phone. My regular phone has a simple voicemail greeting. Google voice either has a generic greeting if I don't have anything for rent, or information about available homes and open house dates. Two numbers, one phone, and no extra cost. It's great!

If I have a phone call I know will involve being on hold for a long time, I will utilize a headset and start the call as I begin a commute, freeing up my radio to listen to music instead of listening to a hold message while driving. When I finally get through to the person

I want to talk to, I cut the radio volume down. No time lost.

This sounds like a lot. Maybe it's tempting to hire all this stuff out and use a property manager. It's up to you, but if you are using a no money down technique to buy your houses and make your student loan payments, you may not be able to afford a property manager. It is customary for property managers to take 10% of the rent they collect, and to take a percentage (sometimes 100%) of the first month's rent as a leasing fee. If your property manager gets a re-leasing fee every time they sign up a new tenant, their motivation may be to re-rent the house every year. Your place could be empty a month out of the year for turnover and make ready, and you could lose another month's rent for your lease up fee. Also, a property manager will use their own resources to repair your place, deduct that from the rent received, and pay you the remainder (if there is any).

Let's say your house rents for $600.00/month:

Property managed: Annual Rent: $600.00 x12 = $7,200.00.

Lease up fee -$600.00

One month empty -$600.00

10% management fee on remaining 10 months, -$600.00.

You just spent $1,800.00 (25% of your rental income!) for someone to answer the phone (that's per house, I have seven). And you have far less tax deductions you can take on your property if someone else manages it. I'll answer my own simple phone calls. Nobody wants to talk to their landlord. Did you want to talk to yours when you were renting a place? Most months I get two or three total calls between my seven houses - at reasonable hours (and it's rare for a call to actually be a big deal). My phone goes into nighttime shutdown mode at 9 p.m. If someone calls or texts after 9 p.m. I get back to them at 5 a.m. when I wake up and check any messages.

Emergency situations are rare. When we sign a lease I tell my tenants, "If the house is on fire and you can't safely use the fire extinguisher, RUN!" Nothing much can be done about fire. The second biggest emergency possible is a pipe bursting. So, the day we sign the lease, I give my new tenant a water shut off key as a gift. Then we do the flood drill. I turn on the kitchen faucet to simulate a broken pipe. Then we walk to the curb. My new tenant has to pull the meter lid off, find the water shut off valve and use the water shut off key to turn it closed. We walk back inside to the kitchen to see that the water is off and I say, "You have now turned an emergency into an urgency. I'm an hour out if you have a pipe break, if you do nothing all your stuff will be flooded by the time I get here. Instead, shut your water off, then call me. I'll have a plumber out first thing in the morning." This has worked for me before. I didn't even have to get out of bed.

Replacing carpet is expensive; there are ways to make it last a little longer. If your carpet is good, except a seam or two is coming apart at a doorway, you can put flat metal transition strips over the seams. The metal strips look natural and only cost a few dollars. Plus, if you need to replace the carpet in a heavily trafficked room, the metal strips create a quick border for an easy installation. The rest of the house is good for a couple of more years. I would rather have hard surface flooring at all my houses, and I love the ones that boast this feature. With hard surface flooring, all you need is a quick mop between tenants and you're done.

A good many landlords have at least one Limited Liability Company (LLC). As the name implies, this type of company has limited legal liabilities. In the event of a lawsuit, a properly maintained LLC can only be sued for what it contains. So, if you have an uninsured roofer working on your house and he falls, he can only sue your company, not you. A huge lawsuit could potentially get all your properties and the money in your rental accounts, but not come after you personally. Some landlords put each house they own in its own company. That means each house has to have its own corporate documents (not hard to do) and its own checking account.

Insurance on a rental house is usually called a "Fire Policy". As the name implies, the policy is designed to kick in if your house is destroyed. A Fire policy is different from a regular Homeowner's policy because it does not insure contents. If your rental burns to the ground, your tenant doesn't get a dollar. If you are investing in cheap properties and want to cut down on overhead, then you would likely insure your house for

120

replacement cost. The homes I buy cost around $30.00 per square foot, and to cheaply build a house today costs $85.00 per square foot, so I insure for the former amount and my insurance bills are less than a third of what they could be. If one of my rentals gets totaled, I'll buy another one nearby instead of rebuilding on the same lot. Each policy runs about $50.00 per month per house.

The lease I use says that the tenant must carry renter's insurance. I include a flyer and business card from my insurance agent as part of my move-in packet. If something untoward should happen, my insurance agent could coordinate my policy and my tenant's policy to help me out as much as possible. I point out to my tenants that their stuff is not insured by my policy, and that a renter's policy protects their possessions everywhere, not just in their house. I point out, "If your laptop gets stolen out of your friend's car, you are covered."

An umbrella policy insures an individual in case of a lawsuit. Usually tied to your car insurance, you can add an umbrella policy for a nominal fee of $15.00-$30.00 a month for $1,000,000.00 - $2,000,000.00 of coverage. If someone steps in a hole in the yard of one of your rent houses and has pain and suffering, you might be the target of a lawsuit, which is also a good reason to hold your properties in a LLC. I've heard a couple different opinions regarding an umbrella policy. The first line of thought is you will have peace of mind against lawsuits. An umbrella policy covers you for more than just landlording. It would also cover you if your kid blinds someone during a soccer game, or whatever else you can imagine. The other line of thought is an umbrella policy makes you a target for a frivolous lawsuit. I don't know how a sleazy lawyer can figure out that someone has coverage, but where there's an ill gotten buck, there's a way. You have to boost your coverage to $300,000.00/$500,000.00/$300,000.00 on your car insurance in order to get an additional umbrella policy.

I use a small PO Box near my home for my rentals. It only costs $50.00 per year and I believe it helps put forth a more professional image. All your other bills go to a PO Box, so why not rent? Plus, I don't really want to advertise where I live. The PO Box section of my local post office is open 24 hours but this is not the case with all post offices. The first PO Box I had was locked every time the post office was closed. I didn't realize how many Sundays and federal holidays there were in a month, nor did I realize how irritating it was to try and scoot across town to fight for a parking spot in a crowded lot before the post office closed at 5pm. Make sure you will have 24 hour access, even if you don't think it's necessary, trust me, it's nice.

You will wear a lot of hats if you become a landlord. Skills will develop over time, but as your empire grows, so must your abilities. I am a homeowner, repairman (as little as possible), accountant, marketing agent, idea man, exterminator, home inspector, document generator, bill collector, private investigator, banker, tough guy, nice guy, paralegal, negotiator, and cheerleader. With only one rental property, bookkeeping and communications are quite simple. As you gain more real estate, your computer becomes more necessary. I use QuickBooks™, Microsoft Excel™, and most of all, Microsoft Word™ on a regular basis.

Like most of life's endeavors, some days suck as a landlord. However, most days are good, and plenty are quite fantastic. Never has there been a day that I regret landlording, it has simply become part of me. Organize yourself, streamline your systems, and be proactive. Your phone will ring less, you will have more personal time, and your rental income will be steady.

Chapter 20: The End?

My little company is on cruise control. It mostly runs by itself, all I have to do is steer a little. Money is direct deposited into, or auto drafted from, various accounts. If I get a phone call about a problem, I send a text message and it gets taken care of.

There are eight years' worth of student loan payments left for us to honor. Nonetheless, I don't even think about my student loans, they are simply a bill my company takes care of, that heavy burden is completely gone. I have no doubt the real estate in my possession will cover every single payment. That mission is accomplished, so now what?

On one hand, landlording has given me a lot more reasons to be happy with my career. I can smile at work even on a bad day, because I have something else going for me besides a job. Plus, my career is what allows me to get money from the bank. The income from my job speaks to the bankers for me, so going to work every day serves a dual purpose. I'm not concerned whether Social Security will exist or not when I hit retirement age. I contribute a lot to my 403b plan because it would be dumb not to, and I get a much needed tax break. But a standard retirement plan will pale in comparison to what I can pull down with rent houses when I decide to retire. Our future is very bright, but blurry.

On the other hand, I still have to go to work *every day*. By doing some simple math I figure if I owned 20 rentals outright (fully paid off) I would never *have* to go to work again. Now, buying 20 houses may seem like a tremendous endeavor to someone new to this game, but when you already have seven, it's not that big of a step.

20 houses x $600.00 per month (what I can net after expenses) = $12,000.00 per month of passive income. I could live off that, or buy another rental every few months. I know people who own 100.

I'm not saying I want to spend my days sitting on my couch staring slack jawed at a TV. But I have the potential to get the rest of my life back. To choose what I do with my day every day. Hell, every weekday I go to work at the nicest part of the day. Daytime! I love having days off in the middle of the week, don't you? There's no traffic, no lines at the store, its quiet outside when everyone is inside - at work. More of that wouldn't be a bad thing... Right?

You don't see TV shows about the landlord business. House flipping shows are exciting and dramatic. Everyone yells, things go horribly wrong, then the show concludes highlighting simple math with huge profits. There is no equivalent for landlords as we don't do very much. Landlording is not flashy or intense, and the money moves slowly and steadily. I find landlording quite exciting from time to time, but nothing happens to me that's reality TV worthy. There are shows on TV that *feature* landlords, and one of those shows is usually on when I eat lunch at work. It films people buying 15,000 square foot homes in exotic locations around the world. The series presents the prospective buyers with three properties to choose from. We watch buyers having to make hard decisions debating, "Well, the one on the beach is listed for $3.4 million, so we will have a lot of room in our budget for renovations, or we could go with the private island for $6.8 million that's move in ready." "Yes dear, and the island house comes with a float plane, you know how I like those." "Okay, we'll take the island." I eat lunch with doctors who gawk at the TV and say, "Who the heck can afford that? What the hell do they do for a living?" I'll bet you a Section 8 payment that I know exactly what they do for a living.

A year after I met my banker we were having lunch together. She said, "I've been in this business since the 1980's, and I've had a lot of people walk into my office. After five minutes of talking to you, I knew I was in the presence of a guy who will be doing million dollar deals someday."

Man, talk about getting a warm fuzzy feeling!

Things have gone differently than I expected. And it's been awesome!

I'm not sure where landlording is going to take us exactly, but paying off a few hundred thousand of student loan debt is only just the beginning.

Here's a final road map for you:

- Find your local real estate investor's group and start going to meetings.
- Straighten out your student loan payments.
- Keep Reading!
  - "Landlording on Autopilot" is a fantastic book and it will provide you with tons of forms and documents.
  - If you don't have money, read "Nothing Down for the 2000's."
  - To hammer home the concept of cash flow and real estate, read "Rich Dad, Poor Dad." People in your real estate group will look at you funny if you haven't already read it anyway.
  - If LLC formation seems complicated, read "NOLOs LLC." Open up a checking account for your LLC.
- Examine your local rental market (I love using Zillow Rentals). What do houses cost compared to how much rent they earn? Look at how much it will cost you to make payments and estimate 10% of your rental income will be used for repairs. Make sure there will still be some money left over. Use this financial data to write up a business plan.

- Find a realtor through your REIA group or by calling around.
- Look at lots of houses, then buy one of them and get it rented. Your first deal will be your hardest and most rewarding. Repeat this process as needed. Soon you will find yourself going to closing for the cookies.
- Continue to network and talk to people. It's amazing who you will meet.

That's all I've got. The ball is now in your court, and I've put it in a sweet spot. Don't be a slave to your student loans. Start your adventure, and find someone else to pay off that debt. Good luck!

Bibliography

1. Allen, Robert, Nothing Down for tl New York, NY: Free Press, 2004.

2. Kiyosaki, Robert, Rich Dad, Poor Dad. New York, NY: Hachette Book Group, 1998.

3. Butler, Mike, Landlording on Auto-Pilot. Hoboken, NJ: John Wiley and Sons, 2006.

4. Mancuso, Anthony, NOLO's Quick LLC. Brainerd, MN: Bang Printing, 2015.

5. Velvel, Salman, Mobile Home Wealth. Garden City Park, NY: Square One Publishers, 2008.

Wait!

Before you go, please take a few seconds to rate this book and fill out a review. I welcome your feedback. Even if you didn't like my book, common decency says you should give it five stars for being terrible. I really want this book to reach the right people, help get them on the path to financial freedom, and overcome their staggering debt. The more reviews this book receives, the more people it will reach. I hope you enjoyed reading this book, I really enjoyed writing it!

Made in the USA
San Bernardino, CA
04 May 2018